THE
ENTREPRENEURIAL
MINDSET

THE ENTREPRENEURIAL MINDSET

PREPARING OUR NEXT GENERATION
FOR THE FUTURE OF WORK

KYLE GARMAN

NDP

NEW DEGREE PRESS

THE ENTREPRENEURIAL MINDSET
*Preparing Our Next Generation
For The Future Of Work*

ISBN
978-1-64137-526-9   *Paperback*
978-1-64137-527-6   *Kindle Ebook*
978-1-64137-528-3   *Digital Ebook*

This book is dedicated to the hundreds of thousands of hard-working people that have been involved with the Network for Teaching Entrepreneurship (NFTE) since it was founded in 1987. NFTE is a nonprofit organization based in New York City that has reached over 1 million students through project-based entrepreneurship education.

Through its network of teachers, volunteers, corporate partners, donors, and alumni, NFTE ignites and develops the Entrepreneurial Mindset in students. One hundred percent of the proceeds from this book are being donated directly to NFTE to support its mission.

CONTENTS

WHAT PEOPLE
ARE SAYING

———

"The world is changing at a pace unlike anything we have witnessed in human history. What kind of mindset is needed to thrive in the 21st century? How can this mindset be developed? Kyle's book provides profound answers to these questions. I urge everyone to read it."

**Diana Davis Spencer, Executive Chairman,
Diana Davis Spencer Foundation**

"We are seeing a realignment of the sorts of competencies and educational experiences that are most valuable for the future of work. *The Entrepreneurial Mindset* is full of insights about why—and how—education must adapt accordingly."

**Peter Walker, Senior Partner Emeritus, McKinsey
& Co. and Author of *Powerful Different Equal***

"Kyle and I are both dreamers with a deep belief in the power of customer-driven innovation. As a former teenage entrepreneur, I'm thrilled that Kyle wrote *The Entrepreneurial Mindset* and encourage everyone to read it."

Bill McDermott, CEO, ServiceNow
and Author of *Winners Dream*

"Kyle and I share a passion for igniting *The Entrepreneurial Mindset* in young people because we see first-hand how entrepreneurship education changes the trajectories of their lives. Kyle's book is an important resource for everyone looking to prepare for the future of work."

Ajay Agarwal, Partner, Bain Capital Ventures
and National Board Chair, BUILD.Org

"I never imagined that my journey as an entrepreneur would lead to becoming Chief Transformation Officer of the United States Air Force. But technology is advancing exponentially, and entrepreneurial thinking is therefore essential across every domain of the private and public sector, including the defense of our nation. Kyle's book provides the formula for developing *The Entrepreneurial Mindset* early and often. I recommend it for everyone."

Lauren Knausenberger, Chief Transformation
Officer, United States Air Force

"I wasn't a natural-born entrepreneur myself but learned I could change my mindset and go about acquiring the skills needed to be successful as an entrepreneur. I love that *The Entrepreneurial Mindset* breaks it down into 8 domains that can be learned, measured, and improved through project-based entrepreneurship education."

David Blake, Founding CEO, Degreed and Managing Partner, Future of Work Studios

"After 25 years in teaching, I embraced project-based entrepreneurship education because I wanted to help students build the mindset they need for the future. This required that I modify my teaching method to be more of a 'Guide on the Side' than a 'Sage on Stage'. The results have been life-changing for my students. Kyle's book is a must-read."

Sandra Cruz, Youth Entrepreneurship Educator, Thomas A. Edison Career and Technical Education High School in Queens, New York

"A masterpiece for the 21st century."

Steve Mariotti, Founder, Network for Teaching Entrepreneurship

"At EY, we know entrepreneurial thinkers are key to building a better working world which is why we evaluate the mindset when we hire. Kyle's book makes a compelling case for why project-based entrepreneurship education is vital to enable the next generation to develop this mindset."

Mike Kacsmar, Partner, Ernst & Young LLP

"Today's—and tomorrow's—leaders must have a mindset geared for continuous innovation and constant re-invention. Kyle's book shows young people how to build *The Entrepreneurial Mindset* now to prepare for the 21st century economy."

Rebecca Zucker, Founding Partner at Next Step Partners and Harvard Business Review Contributor

"Kyle and I share a belief that bringing mentors from the business world together with students through project-based entrepreneurship education is a critical aspect of equipping young people for the 21st century. I encourage everyone looking to help the next generation develop the mindset required for the future of work to read this book."

Patty Alper, Author of *Teach to Work: How a Mentor, A Mentee and a Project Can Close The Skills Gap in America*

"Project-based entrepreneurship education empowers young people with the skills and experience to broaden their worldview and their belief in what's possible. I experienced this first-hand growing up, and I'm a firm believer that this is a terrific investment in the success of the next generation as Kyle's book demonstrates."

Ryan Williams, Founder & CEO, Cadre

"*The Entrepreneurial Mindset* is more than a book. It's a blueprint for change that schools can adopt now to prepare students for the 21st century. I strongly recommend Kyle's book for everyone involved at the intersection of education and the future of work."

Matt Greenfield, Managing Partner, Re-Think Education

"The beauty of teaching project-based entrepreneurship is that it's never about me. It's about pushing my students to discover their interests and then using my experience to coach them through the process of turning that into a solution that has real value. Kyle's book illustrates how powerful this is."

Ray Parris, Youth Entrepreneurship Educator and Department Head of Digital Media and Entrepreneurship at Hialeah Miami-Lakes Senior High School in Florida

"A pioneering prescription for developing young innovators for the 21st century."

Dan Mindus, Founder & Managing Partner, NextGen Venture Partners

"Following a 20-year career in business, I began searching for the best way to give back to the next generation. I found it through project-based entrepreneurship education. Kyle's book reveals how empowering it is when students develop *The Entrepreneurial Mindset* prior to adulthood. I urge you to read it."

Angela Miceli, Youth Entrepreneurship Educator, Holy Trinity High School in Chicago, IL

"*The Entrepreneurial Mindset* brings to light the value of entrepreneurship as a required learning experience to prepare students for the world. I know first-hand, because I was a teenager whose life was changed by the simple act of learning how to create a business. Project-based entrepreneurship is a game changer, particularly for the most under-served students. Here's hoping that Kyle's book starts a movement."

Kimberly Smith, Executive Director of the League of Innovative Schools, Digital Promise

"One of the key ingredients for enabling students to transition into a career they enjoy is empowering them to pursue their interests early on. Project-based entrepreneurship education is a fantastic way to do that. *The Entrepreneurial Mindset* provides the playbook."

Pete Wheelan, CEO, InsideTrack and Executive Chairman, Roadtrip Nation

"*The Entrepreneurial Mindset* is a must-read for anyone interested in education."

Kevin Capitani, Former President, Pearson North America and National Board Director Reading Partners

"Project-based entrepreneurship in schools is an idea whose time has come, as *The Entrepreneurial Mindset* showcases. As a component of learning, it has much to offer students preparing for their future."

Michael Horn, Author of *Choosing College* and Co-Founder of the Clayton Christensen Institute

"I applaud Kyle for assembling such a powerful and inclusive collection of voices around one of the most urgent imperatives of the 21st century—how do we prepare young people for the future of work? *The Entrepreneurial Mindset* shows us how."

Rahim Fazal, Co-Founder & CEO, SVAcademy

ACKNOWLEDGMENTS

I want to acknowledge my beautiful wife of nearly twenty years Jennifer Garman for being the love of my life and the source of my strength in seeing this project through. I would also like to thank my three wonderful children Jordan, Caden, and Emery for inspiring me every day to be the best father and person I can be. In addition, I want to thank my mom for her ever-present unconditional love, and my dad who showed me that a purpose-driven life is a meaningful life.

Finally, I would like to acknowledge the following individuals for their contributions to the development, production, and promotion of this book in alphabetical order as follows:

Ajay Agarwal	Katie Booth
Patty Alper	Peter Boni
Michael Beas	Amanda Brown
Brien Bies	Kevin Capitani
Lauren Bailey	Lisa Chalmers
Meagan Baier	Gina Champagne
Linda Beradelli	Stephanie Cirami
David Blake	Tara Coburn

Obinno Coley
Sandra Cruz
Zoe Damacela
Jason Delgatto
Atle Erlingsson
Ruthe Farmer
Rahim Fazal
Julie Friedman
Juan Daniel Ramos Fuentes
Dagim Girma
Thomas Gold
Matt Greenfield
Caitlin Griffin
John Gurski
Victoria Haler
Nick Hare
Tamas Hevizi
Michael Horn
Jim Johnston
Mike Kacsmar
Alok Kapur
Mitch Kick
Lauren Knausenberger
Eric Koester
Milan Krstevski
Erin LaBarge
J.D. LaRock
Brittany Lothe
Stefan Mancevski
Steve Mariotti

Bill McDermott
Angela Miceli
Dan Mindus
Josephine Monberg
Nancy Nowlan
Shawn Osbourne
Barclay Oudersluys
D.J. Paoni
Ray Parris
Bryan Pearce
Gjorgji Pejkovski
Alexander Pyles
Mary Radford
Sophia Rodriguez
Keith Schmehl
Gabriel Sheikh
Kaitlyn Smith
Kimberly Smith
Diana Davis Spencer
Ted Thompson
Alicia Tillman
Alex Van Atta
Jon Walker
Peter Walker
Jane Walsh
Heather Wetzler
Pete Wheelan
Ryan Williams
Jonathan Woahn
Rebecca Zucker.

INTRODUCTION

A Silicon Valley software company—Automation Anywhere—is on track to become the world's largest "employer" with over three million digital bots operating as "workers" for its customers.[1]

The CEO of Deutsche Bank has recently suggested that half of its 97,000 employees could be replaced by robots.[2]

Plus.ai, a Silicon Valley self-driving truck company, completed the first cross-country autonomous freight run in the U.S., delivering 40,000 pounds of butter for Land O'Lakes.[3]

Google software defeated the world's best player of the highly complex Chinese game *Go* by "learning" to recognize

---

1   "Automation Anywhere Predicts it will be the World's Largest Digital Employer by 2020, On Track to Deploy Three Million Bots Worldwide."

2   John Detrixhe, "Deutsche Bank's CEO hints that half its workers could be replaced by machines."

3   "Plus.ai Completes First Cross-Country Commercial Freight Run by a Self-Driving Truck in Record Three Days."

patterns at a level that humans could not match.[4] Similar methods are now being applied to fields including medicine, law, and finance.[5]

Within the governmental apparatus, The Defense Advanced Research Projects Agency in the U.S. is experimenting with swarms of autonomous drones and ground robots to remotely execute military operations.[6]

All around us, we see that exponentially advancing technology is reshaping every corner of our economy and society. The pace of change is breathtaking. And it's unprecedented.

Global threats ranging from COVID-19[7] to climate change are exacerbating the disruption.[8] At the present moment Volatility, Uncertainty, Complexity, and Ambiguity (VUCA) presides as our new normal.[9] It has become ominously clear that the Future of Work in the twenty-first century will look profoundly different than the past.[10]

---

4   Cade Metz, "Google's AlphaGo Levels Up from Board Games to Power Grids."

5   Sam McRoberts, "Artificial Intelligence Is Likely to Make a Career in Finance, Medicine or Law a Lot Less Lucrative."

6   Jay Peters, "Watch DARPA test out swarms of drones."

7   Borge Brende, "COVID-19 Pandemic Shows We Must Reduce Our Blindspot to Risk."

8   David Introcaso, "Climate Change Is The Greatest Threat To Human Health in History."

9   Sunnie Giles, "How VUCA Is Reshaping The Business Environment, And What It Means For Innovation."

10   Singularity University, "Future of Work | Singularity U Spain Summit 2019."

As the father of three children, a member of the board of directors of the Network for Teaching Entrepreneurship (NFTE), and an executive in the technology industry, I have asked myself three questions nearly every day for the last several years:

1. What kind of mindset is needed to thrive in the Future of Work?

2. What is the best way for young people to build this mindset?

3. How can we scale this mindset development as broadly as possible?

The stakes involved in answering these questions could not be any higher. If we get these answers right, we can usher in a new age of prosperity in which humans and intelligent machines collaborate in novel ways that bring immeasurable benefits to humanity. On the flip side, if we get it wrong vast portions of our next generations could get locked out of our economy, resulting in even more extreme inequality and instability.

Many proclaim that Science, Technology, Engineering, and Math (STEM) is the answer to equip young people for the future. Without a doubt, STEM education is critical given the central role that these disciplines play in our modern economy.[11] However, STEM alone is not enough to prepare students for the new frontier ahead.

---

11   "Why Is STEM Education So Important?"

Consider how the two sides of the human brain are depicted in popular culture. While the portrayal is not scientifically accurate, it does provide a useful image for visualizing a balanced view of human aptitudes.[12]

The left brain is commonly associated with methodical functions often encapsulated in STEM. This is exactly where exponentially improving intelligent machines excel. Job functions consisting of repetitive tasks or pattern recognition are likely to be automated, and probably sooner rather than later.[13]

Then there is the right brain, which elicits our capacities for creativity, imagination, social intelligence, complex human collaboration, and holistic problem solving. These capabilities are far more difficult for intelligent machines to replicate.[14]

As such, it is incumbent on us to play to our uniquely human strengths by adapting our educational systems to focus more on these right-brain competencies. In light of relentlessly progressing technology, these are precisely the sorts of proficiencies that have become most desirable to employers.[15]

Research has shown that teaching entrepreneurship through project-based learning tied to each student's

---

12 "Left Brain vs. Right Brain: What Does This Mean for Me?"

13 "Future of Work | Singularity U Spain Summit 2019."

14 Ibid.

15 Alex Gray, "The 10 skills you need to thrive in the Fourth Industrial Revolution."

individual interests imbues these distinctly human faculties in remarkably beneficial ways.[16] While some students become inspired to start their own businesses, this is not necessarily the primary goal. Rather, the aim is to develop the Entrepreneurial Mindset in young learners so they are empowered to flourish in the twenty-first century, regardless of the career paths they choose now and at later life junctures.

The Entrepreneurial Mindset is defined as a set of attitudes, behaviors, and skills characterized by eight core domains as follows:[17]

1. Future Orientation

2. Creativity & Innovation

3. Comfort with Risk

4. Communication & Collaboration

5. Flexibility & Adaptability

6. Critical Thinking & Problem Solving

7. Initiative & Self-reliance

8. Opportunity Recognition

---

16 "Encouraging Future Innovation: Youth Entrepreneurship Education."

17 "Tools for Life."

In this book, my goal is to answer each of the three questions I raised earlier:

1. First, I contend the Future of Work requires that people develop the Entrepreneurial Mindset.

2. Second, I establish that project-based entrepreneurship education is the quintessential learning method through which to build this mindset.

3. Third, I formulate some organizing principles for enabling the widespread advancement of the Entrepreneurial Mindset for young learners.

IS THIS BOOK FOR YOU?

I realize you are coming at these issues from a wide range of viewpoints. Consider the following four scenarios:

1. You are looking to calibrate your mindset for a world being transformed by exponential change.

2. You are a parent, grandparent, or concerned citizen who sees how technology and global threats are altering our world, and you are seeking ways to empower young people for the twenty-first century economy.

3. You are an educator, administrator, school board leader, or education policy maker searching for pedagogies that are designed to bolster students' prospects in consideration of the Future of Work.

4. You are an entrepreneur, investor, or leader in the private or public sector interested in developing our next generation of innovators.

If you identify with one or more of these perspectives, this book is for you.

NAVIGATING THIS BOOK

In order to facilitate your reading experience, I have provided a summary below to help you navigate this book. It is organized into ten chapters as follows:

1. **Chapter 1** illustrates how the trajectories of three young people's lives were changed forever as a result of project-based entrepreneurship education. These firsthand, real-life stories provide a glimpse of how powerful it is when the Entrepreneurial Mindset is ignited in students prior to adulthood.

2. **Chapter 2** explains how a visit with my wife and three kids to an Audi factory run by robots in Germany was the pivotal moment that led me to write this book.

3. **Chapter 3** examines three precepts underpinning the original design of our public K-12 educational systems in the U.S., which arose in the mid-nineteenth century in order to accelerate Industrialization.[18] These axioms include a presumption of knowledge scarcity vs. knowledge abundance,[19]

---

18   Jim Chappelow, "What is Industrialization?"

19   Daniel Araya, *Rethinking US Education Policy: Paradigms of the Knowledge Economy*, 116.

an emphasis on convergent thinking vs. divergent thinking,[20] and a focus on preparation for performing repetitive tasks.[21] This historical context provides useful insights for contemplating readjustments to our educational systems and pedagogical ideals looking forward.

4. **Chapter 4** analyzes three trends shaping the Future of Work in the twenty-first century. These dynamics include the automation of repetitive tasks and pattern recognition,[22] the rise of the Gig Economy whereby work is increasingly performed remotely[23] by independent contractors,[24] and the emergence of Conscious Capitalism in which winning companies focus on social good alongside maximizing profits for shareholders.[25] These forces are resulting in a realignment of the kinds of skills and educational experiences that are most valuable moving forward.

5. **Chapter 5** explores the eight domains of the Entrepreneurial Mindset and reveals how this ethos enables people to become "robot-proof"[26] for the Future of Work.

---

20 Sergey Markov, "Joy Paul Guilford–One of the founders of the Psychology of Creativity."

21 Alvin Toffler, *Future Shock*, 398-427.

22 "Future of Work | Singularity U Spain Summit 2019."

23 Maurie Backman, "Could COVID-19 Cause a Permanent Shift to Remote Work?"

24 "Best Gig Economy Apps: 50 Leading Apps to Find Gig Work and Live the Gig Economy Lifestyle."

25 John Mackey and Raj Sisodia, *Conscious Capitalism*, Chap. 1-2.

26 Joseph E. Aoun, *Robot-Proof: Higher Education in the Age of Artificial Intelligence*, Chap. 1.

Here you will find descriptions, examples, and more depth behind each of the eight elements.

6. **Chapter 6** articulates how the eight domains of the Entrepreneurial Mindset are measured and monitored for continuous improvement. Just as the SAT and other standardized tests are designed to evaluate certain academic skills, this assessment quantifies a student's propensity for entrepreneurial thinking.[27]

7. **Chapter 7** demonstrates how the project-based entrepreneurship pedagogy is uniquely designed to help young people develop the Entrepreneurial Mindset.[28] This material is conveyed through the eyes of the curriculum's architects.

8. **Chapter 8** showcases how the business planning project in entrepreneurship education is an ideal means to connect young learners to the "real world" early and often through mentor relationships. The network effects resulting from external collaboration around business plans are a key factor that makes this pedagogy so well-suited for building the Entrepreneurial Mindset.

9. **Chapter 9** chronicles the stories of four heroic teachers of youth entrepreneurship, including the founder of NFTE, Steve Mariotti. If you want to be inspired by the true stories of some real-life heroes, this chapter is for you.

---

27   Gold and Rodriguez, "Measuring Entrepreneurial Mindset In Youth: Learnings From NFTE's Entrepreneurial Mindset Index."

28   "How we do it."

10. **Chapter 10** formulates seven tenets for organizing the proliferation of project-based entrepreneurship education for young learners across the U.S., while giving some consideration to international factors as well.

Immediately following Chapter 10 is a Glossary of defined terms. If you find yourself looking for a concise definition of a capitalized term in the book, the Glossary is a quick and easy way to locate it.

I'd like to conclude this introduction with a quote from Nelson Mandela who said, "Education is the most powerful weapon which you can use to change the world."[29] Imagine the impact we can have on the trajectories of young people's lives by imparting the Entrepreneurial Mindset prior to adulthood.

As you will see throughout this book, the Future of Work necessitates that we enrich every young learner in this way through project-based entrepreneurship education. The future of our nation, our society, and indeed our world is counting on you to join the movement to make this vision a reality.

---

29   Valerie Strauss, "Nelson Mandela on the power of education."

CHAPTER 1

ALTERING TRAJECTORIES

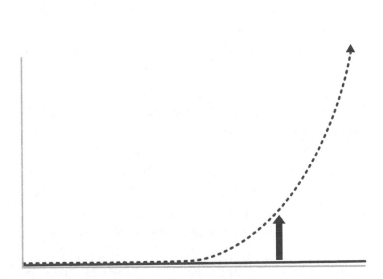

Have you ever watched *Shark Tank* on TV?

If so, you have probably seen how successfully presenting a compelling business idea to a panel of influential judges can change the progression of one's life. Contestants on the show often spend hundreds of hours rehearsing for the high-stakes moment of pitching their business plans to celebrities such as Daymond John, Mark Cuban, and Barbara Corcoran.

For young people, these sorts of competitions are frequently the galvanizing force that synthesizes the various aspects of the project-based entrepreneurship educational experience.[30] Finalists receive prize money to advance their business ideas and assist with their pursuit of higher education. More importantly, for those that earnestly put in the work, the Entrepreneurial Mindset becomes an integral part of their ethos before they reach adulthood.

To illustrate the impact that project-based entrepreneurship education can have on the arc of young people's lives, let's explore the real-life stories of Zoe Damacela, Dagim Girma, and Gabriel Sheikh. All three were finalists in the Youth Entrepreneurship Challenge that sees thousands of high school students compete at local and regional levels across the U.S. each year in a bid to reach the national finals in New York City.[31]

As you will see, the experience altered the trajectories of their lives.

---

30 Kayla Prochnow, "The Best Entrepreneurship Competitions for K-12 Students."

31 "Youth Entrepreneurship Challenge."

THE LAUNCH PAD

Walking up the stairs to the podium at center stage of the Northwestern University Center in downtown Chicago, sixteen-year-old Zoe Damacela's heart was racing. She was terrified of public speaking. But here she was about to present her business plan for Zoe Damacela Apparel to a panel of judges consisting of some of Chicago's most prominent business leaders and an audience of hundreds of onlookers.

She began her presentation by asking the women in the audience to raise their hands if they had difficulty finding the right clothing for special occasions. A hand from every female in the room shot up. Damacela could not possibly have imagined the sequence of events that was about to change her life forever.

Raised in poverty by a single mother on Chicago's South Side, Damacela knew firsthand how difficult it was to make ends meet. Her mother shifted from one minimum wage job to another and did her best to make sure Damacela had a roof over her head and food on the table.

After school each day, Damacela always went straight to day care because her mother worked long hours and was not available for her until late in the evening. Although she missed her mother terribly each evening, her mom explained that her long hours were necessary for their survival and Damacela understood.

She recalls a moment at age eight when the poverty in which she grew up hit her. Some other kids had brought Razor scooters to school and were having a grand time playing outside before the bell rang.

"I saw those scooters and I wanted to have one so badly," Damacela said. When her mom came home from work late that evening, she asked if she could get one for her birthday.

But when she revealed that it would cost $60, her mom said that she simply could not afford it. "At that moment," Damacela said, "I became determined to find a way to earn $60 so I could buy myself a scooter." Her creative mind began to churn.

Since her birthday was coming up, she thought about selling personalized birthday cards so others could give them to their loved ones on their special days. Damacela set up her own version of a lemonade stand on the front porch of her apartment. She asked those passing by to identify any family birthdays that were around the corner.

She also inquired about what kinds of messages would make each person feel appreciated on their big days. Damacela sold $40 worth of cards in one day and then successfully negotiated with her mom to chip in the rest for her Razor scooter. The seeds of a budding entrepreneur had been planted.

In seventh grade, Damacela chose to take an elective class in sewing. As a pre-teen, her interest in clothing was growing, and she was curious about how clothes were manufactured.

She began viewing YouTube videos to learn about clothing design. As she watched, she became fascinated with the thought process that went into deciding what kinds of clothes people wanted to wear.

Soon thereafter, Damacela began developing her own unique designs and sewing her clothing by hand. When she showed her designs to her friends, they wanted to purchase them.

* * *

By her sophomore year at Whitney Young High School in Chicago, Damacela was immersed in her newfound passion for designing, manufacturing, and selling clothes. In reviewing elective courses for her upcoming junior year in the fall of 2009, an entrepreneurship class caught her attention. She signed up and was excited to learn what it was all about.

The first day of class, Damacela noticed that project-based entrepreneurship education was very different than other classes she had taken. "Our teacher, Ms. Kane, asked us to think about something that we were interested in as opposed to summarizing the syllabus for the course," Damacela told me. Further, Ms. Kane said that there would be no formal test to determine the grade for the course.

Instead, students would be assessed on a business plan they would create and present to a panel of judges. Immediately, Damacela knew this would be an opportunity to build upon her interest in fashion.

In the weeks and months that followed, Damacela felt a sense of empowerment that she had not previously known. The process of translating her passion for clothing design into an actual business plan propelled her to think more deeply about the industry and how to carve her own unique niche within it.

She segmented her target customers, refined her competitive advantage, quantified unit economics, crafted a marketing plan, and imagined what the future could look like in three to five years. Those first entrepreneurial instincts within her—the ones she had first become aware of by selling birthday cards to buy a scooter at age eight—were flourishing.

Damacela earned top scores in the initial rounds of the local business plan competition. Then the day arrived for her to present Zoe Damacela Apparel at the regional finals on stage in downtown Chicago at the Northwestern University Center.

She nailed the presentation. Damacela placed first at the event and qualified for the national competition in New York City.

One of the judges on the panel in Chicago was so impressed with Damacela that he decided to run a story about her in *Crain's Chicago Business*, a widely circulated business publication.[32] This led to multiple TV appearances, including her debut on the nationally syndicated *Tyra Banks Show*.[33] Banks was so enamored with Damacela that she agreed to become her mentor, promote her clothing line through

---

32   *Crain's Chicago Business*, "Zoe Damacela: An entrepreneur is born."

33   "Zoe Damacela on the *Tyra Banks Show*."

social media, and sponsor her to be featured on the cover of *Seventeen Magazine*.[34]

Moreover, following her presentation at nationals in New York City she was invited to meet with President Obama at the White House.[35] In just one year, Damacela had gone from a shy teenager who was petrified of public speaking to appearing on national TV with Tyra Banks and meeting with the President of the United States at the White House!

Damacela went on to attend Northwestern University and in 2014, she became the first person in her family to graduate from college. She successfully sold off Zoe Damacela Apparel and managed to fit in internships during the summers in college. Ultimately, she concluded that she could achieve more by joining Macy's as a designer in New York City as opposed to starting another venture independently.

Today, Damacela is the lead designer behind Bar III, one of the fastest growing and most successful clothing lines at Macy's. The brand targets women in the twenty-five to thirty-five age range with clothing that is stylish enough to wear to work, yet comfortable enough to wear socially in the evening. Damacela credits the development of her Entrepreneurial Mindset through project-based entrepreneurship education in high school as the single most important factor for her success with her own business, and as a designer at Macy's.

---

34 Ann Shoket, "Introducing the First Ever Cover Reader Star!"

35 "Winners of NFTE National Youth Entrepreneurship Competition Meet President Obama."

The entrepreneurship competition that she entered as a six-teen-year-old high school student was the launchpad for her extraordinary achievements.

THE GAME CHANGER

Have you ever seen the movie *Remember the Titans?*

If you are an American football fan, you are probably familiar with it. In the film, Academy Award-winning actor Denzel Washington plays the role of head football coach at T.C. Williams High School in Alexandria, Virginia. The scene is 1971, when three segregated schools merged into one larger institution: T.C. Williams. Washington's character plays the heroic role of fighting through scathing racial tensions on the team to ultimately lead them to the state title.[36]

It's an inspiring story based on the actual events of these young athletes joining forces to achieve something bigger than sports. By demonstrating their commitment to each other and their common goal, the team showed us the power of people of coming together irrespective of their differences.

It turns out that T.C. Williams High School produced another inspiring story, one that you probably have not yet heard about. Dagim Girma was born in Alexandria, Virginia shortly after his mother and father immigrated to the area from rural Ethiopia in 1996 in search of a better life for their children. Girma's father got a steady job as an accountant for an association in nearby Washington,

---

36 *Remember the Titans.*

D.C., but adapting to their new environment was a constant struggle for the family.

Growing up, Girma was shy and introverted, cognizant of the cultural disparities that seemed to separate his family from fitting in with their community. At the same time, he began to show entrepreneurial instincts as early as age seven, playing with computers and dabbling with software coding and gaming. As his creative spirit grew in the ensuing years, he recalls thinking that he shouldn't spend so much time on his innovative ideas.

"I never seriously considered turning my creative energy into a business because I always thought you had to wait until adulthood for that," Girma recounted.

By the time he entered high school at T.C. Williams in 2010, Girma had also developed a passion for sports. He explained that when *Remember the Titans* was released in 2000, it generated so much buzz around high school athletics in the area that it was almost impossible not to get caught up in the frenzy.

At T.C. Williams, Girma played both tennis and football. Based on the friendships he formed through athletics, Girma felt connected with his teammates and his surrounding environment for the first time. But the feelings of loneliness and isolation that he had endured in his early years, created a profound sense of empathy for others that he knew still felt this way.

An idea began swirling in Girma's mind that perhaps he could combine his interests in sports, entrepreneurship, and coding in a way that would help other high school students enjoy the same sense of togetherness he had come to know.

But it was not until the day he walked into Ms. Mary Ellen McCormick's project-based entrepreneurship class at the beginning of his junior year that he realized he could turn his concept into a real business.

On the first day, Ms. McCormick asked the class to envision ideas for a project they would each undertake to build a business plan over the course of the year. "From that moment forward," Girma proclaimed, "I knew the time was right for me to let go of playing football, and instead pour my energy into building a company."

Girma called his new business The Audible.

The concept behind The Audible was to bring sports content together with a blogging platform that would allow high school students to write about their opinions on their favorite teams, players, and games. Each blogger would start out as a "rookie" on the website.

Based on the amount of views and commentary they generated from their blogs, students would earn points that would be tracked on the site. Those who generated the highest number of page views would be eligible for the "Audible Hall of Fame." More broadly, participants would become part of The Audible community with sports as their common interest.

* * *

Over the next few months, Girma crafted his business plan to share advertising revenue with other bloggers on the website. Ms. McCormick could see the passion that Girma had for growing the company, so she tapped into her network to connect Girma with local sports industry executives. Through this process, Girma was able to get advice from several high-profile business leaders in the area including Ted Leonsis, CEO of Monumental Sports and owner of sports teams including the NBA's Washington Wizards and the NHL's Washington Capitals.

Toward the end of his junior year, Ms. McCormick encouraged Girma to enter NFTE's business planning competition. Initially, Girma thought it wasn't for him because the idea of presenting his plan on stage in front of an audience was terrifying.

But Ms. McCormick was relentless in using the project-based curriculum to improve his confidence in his communication skills. She arranged for Girma and the other students to practice their pitches repeatedly with each other and share their feedback. Reluctantly, Girma agreed to enter the Youth Entrepreneurship Challenge.

He sailed through the local and regional rounds, earning glowing marks from volunteer business leaders in the D.C. area who served as judges for the competitions. When Girma was notified that his performances qualified him to be one of the top young entrepreneurs to compete in the national finals in New York City in October of 2014, he was ecstatic.

Then came the big day, live on stage at the Times Center in New York City. The event began with a private meeting between each of the three finalists and Sean Combs, the rapper known as P. Diddy. Diddy attended the event to offer encouragement and a few words of advice to the three contestants. Girma was blown away to meet him, but there was no time to reminisce.

Soon thereafter, Girma's name was called as the first presenter of the top three finalists. Walking onto the stage, he recounts that a strange sense of calmness overcame him. By this time, he had rehearsed his pitch literally hundreds of times, collecting new input each time along the way. He knew he was ready for this moment.

When the audience of about 1,000 onlookers rose to their feet and gave him a standing ovation at the end of his presentation, Girma knew he had succeeded. "I remember that feeling of being on stage and hearing the applause like it was yesterday," Girma said with a surge of emotion in his voice. You can view a recording of his pitch on YouTube by typing "Dagim Girma The Audible" into the search box.[37]

After the competition, NFTE founder, Steve Mariotti, pulled Girma aside and mentioned that a university called Babson in Boston could be a great fit for him. Girma was by then a senior and was actively applying to colleges, but he had never heard of the school.

Returning home to Alexandria the next day, Girma could hardly believe what had just happened. He did some research on Babson, and he discovered that it is regarded by many as the premier university in the U.S. for entrepreneurship

---

37   The Audible, "The Audible Final Presentation in New York |
       Dagim Girma."

education. "I would not have known about Babson if it weren't for my experience with the competition," Girma explained. It was immediately clear to him that this was a path he must pursue.

The following day, he received a link to apply for a full scholarship to the university. Girma then reached out to Diana Davis Spencer, one of NFTE's major sponsors who had seen him present at both the D.C. regional finals and the national finals in New York City.

Spencer graciously accepted his request for her to write a letter of recommendation to Babson on his behalf. A few months later, Girma received notice that Babson had admitted him to the university with a full scholarship.

In addition, Girma and the other two finalists were invited to the White House to meet with President Obama, a strong supporter of youth entrepreneurship education. Girma made the short trip across the Potomac River from Alexandria during his senior year to go to the White House.[38]

He was stunned when the President shook his hand and pronounced his name with thoroughly practiced precision. Dagim is pronounced "day-gum" for anyone that may have the opportunity to meet him in the future.

At Babson, Girma had the experience of a lifetime. He was able to grow and learn about all aspects of entrepreneurship from professors and students from all over the world. He

---

38 "Babson Student Named EY Global Youth Entrepreneur of the Year."

studied abroad one semester in Berlin, among many other highlights. As he learned more about entrepreneurship, he discovered that he had a growing interest in the financial side of business, so he took several focused courses on this topic as well.

When it came time to start thinking about his life beyond Babson, Girma broke new ground yet again. He parlayed his newfound interest in finance into an internship at Goldman Sachs, and ultimately accepted a full-time position with the firm. The company had historically not recruited from the school, but they found that Girma's unique experiences and his Entrepreneurial Mindset would be exceptionally valuable as they were looking at entering new market segments.

Today, Girma is a lead digital product manager for the newly formed consumer banking division of Goldman Sachs called Marcus. He has found that building new ventures within an established company can be just as rewarding as starting his own business. And he is tremendously excited about how technology is reshaping the financial services industry.

For Dagim Girma, the competition that he was hesitant to enter during his junior year at T.C. Williams High School was a game changer.

HAVE NO FEAR

What do Americans fear more than anything else?

I'll give you a hint. Dying is number two on the list.

The number one thing that scares people most is…public speaking. In fact, seventy-five percent of the U.S. population reports being afraid of presenting in front of an audience.[39]

This singular trepidation is responsible for preventing countless people from pursuing their dreams because many careers require this skill. Imagine the business opportunity for a young entrepreneur if they could find a way to solve this problem at scale. This is exactly what a sixteen-year-old entrepreneur named Gabriel Sheikh did.

Sheikh grew up in Chicago as the son of a single mother who immigrated to the U.S. at the age of twenty from Poland. As a teenager in Poland, Sheikh's mother Lucyna saw Hollywood movies on TV that showcased America as the land of opportunity.

Struggling to find work in the sluggish Polish economy after completing two years of post-secondary education, Lucyna applied for a U.S. visa through a lottery system. When her number was called, she could hardly believe it.

Despite her fear of the unknown, Lucyna set off for the U.S. in 1990 and settled in Chicago where she found work as a house cleaner and a babysitter. Moving from job to job, she barely managed to make ends meet.

But Lucyna persisted, and eventually she had two children. After Sheikh was born, however, his father suddenly and inexplicably fled the family. Lucyna was left by herself to raise Sheikh and her daughter from a prior relationship.

---

39 "6 Facts About Public Speaking Anxiety."

Lucyna's heart was broken, but her will to raise her two children in the U.S. and enable them to achieve their dreams was unbreakable. She decided that the best way to take care of her kids and earn a living at the same time was to open up a home daycare business.

With virtually no experience managing a business, Lucyna was mocked by her peers who viewed her early entrepreneurial endeavors as an impossible dream. But she proved them wrong. It was relentlessly hard work, but having her own company gave Lucyna a sense of pride and purpose that would have a lasting impact on Sheikh.

* * *

By the time Sheikh entered high school at Holy Trinity in Chicago, he had discovered his own unique talents in math and science. He pursued these subjects vigorously and dreamed of one day having a STEM-oriented career.

"I realized early on that I was well-suited for STEM subjects," Sheikh noted. "But I was quite reserved, meaning I wasn't always the most social person early on in high school"

Sheikh's after-school robotics club turned out to be a perfect program through which he was able to advance his STEM capabilities. He also formed strong friendships with students in the club based upon their shared interests.

At the beginning of his junior year at Holy Trinity, Sheikh enrolled in an entrepreneurship course offered by the school. He was intrigued by the projects created by previous students, but he wasn't sure if he wanted to pursue a business-related field. In fact, he was mainly interested in learning something that could help his mother Lucyna with her home daycare business.

When it came time to determine an idea for his business plan, Sheikh decided to go with a clothing product called the "One Piece Suit." The concept was for young men to have a simple pullover, made up of multiple layers of different fabrics, that looked like a tuxedo when coupled with regular black pants.

A few weeks into the class, Sheikh's teacher, Ms. Angela Miceli, explained that at the end of the course, students would have to present their business plans to their peers and a panel of judges. When hearing about the grand prizes for national finalists, Sheikh was determined to try his best to actualize his business idea.

There was one big problem, though.

Sheikh was terrified of speaking in front of an audience. As time went on, Sheikh began to panic. He found self-help guides online and some apps that record your voice to recommend tone variances. However, there was nothing to address his most debilitating fear—the thought of people scrutinizing every aspect of his visual performance.

Just as his trepidation began to spiral out of control, an idea hit him. "It occurred to me that there must be others that felt this same kind of apprehension," Sheikh told me. "Somehow, I knew there had to be a better way to address this problem."

Sheikh began to envision an app that would use artificial intelligence to improve all aspects of users' presentations. It would capture video of users rehearsing their presentations, quantify their proficiencies in various skills, and generate personalized learning plans to make improvements.

He shared his new concept with Ms. Miceli and her response was overwhelmingly positive. Ms. Miceli was very aware of the struggles that people face with public speaking, and she encouraged Sheikh to go all in with his innovative idea. She also pointed out that this new approach would allow him to take advantage of his STEM skills more than his "One Piece Suit" clothing product.

Sheikh decided to call his new company Presistant, "your smart presentation assistant."

In the ensuing months, Sheikh feverishly developed his business plan and created screenshots of an iPhone app to visualize the user experience. His confidence began to soar as he received positive feedback from classmates and volunteer business leaders that Ms. Miceli arranged to visit the class.

Leading up to the competition, Sheikh practiced his pitch dozens of times in front of a mirror. He was as ready as he could be without the support of the actual Presistant app to aid him.

Sheikh sailed through his initial presentations, advancing from local to regional rounds. After winning first place in the Chicago region, he qualified to compete at the national competition in October of 2019 in New York City.

He spent the summer improving every component of his pitch. Sheikh consulted with computer scientists and engineers to better grasp the possibilities of building Presistant using cloud software platforms. And he worked alongside mentors from Slalom Consulting, who helped him conduct surveys to assess consumer demand and the optimal target market for his business.

Sheikh was ready for his big trip.

I was fortunate to be in the audience that evening for Sheikh's presentation at the Times Center. He crushed it. Sheikh had transformed from an introverted math whiz who was terrified of public speaking into a confident young man with a budding Entrepreneurial Mindset as a result of his educational experience.

As Sheikh now looks toward college, he plans to pursue a major in computer engineering, with a minor in business, continuing with his newfound passion for entrepreneurial thinking. Perhaps the most rewarding part of Sheikh's endeavor was the smile on his mother Lucyna's face as he came off that stage in New York City.

The years of sacrifice Lucyna had made to enable her son to pursue his dreams had paid off, and she was glowing. She now jokingly refers to her son as the next Steve Jobs who just needs to find his Steve Wozniak to help him build Presistant into the next Apple.

It's amazing how big dreams can become when you overcome fear.

CONCLUSION

The real-life examples of Zoe Damacela, Dagim Girma, and Gabriel Sheikh demonstrate how powerful entrepreneurship education is in altering the trajectories of young people's lives. But these transformations did not occur simply because they entered competitions in high school like what you see on *Shark Tank*.

These transformations were the result of project-based entrepreneurship educational experiences that ignited and developed the Entrepreneurial Mindset in each of them, prior to adulthood. Perhaps these stories make you wonder why this sort of educational experience is not offered to more young learners in the U.S. and around the world.

As the father of three children, a board member of the Network for Teaching Entrepreneurship, and an executive in the technology industry, this is something I have thought about extensively. But it was not until a pivotal moment occurred, while I was living in Germany with my family, that I realized this book must be written.

CHAPTER 2

A PIVOTAL MOMENT

—

In each of our lives, we have pivotal moments. Moments where something happens, often unexpectedly, that cause us to see things from a different perspective, pursue a new path, or embrace a powerful sense of purpose. On July 16, 2016, I had one such moment in a small town called Neckarsulm in Germany.

The summer of 2016 was a time of great joy and overwhelming pain for me. I had recently accepted a new global leadership role with my company, SAP, the third largest software company in the world.[40] The position required that I work closely with other executives at our headquarters in Germany, so I made a request for funding to allow for me and my family to live there for the summer which was graciously approved.

My wife Jennifer, our nine-year-old twins Jordan and Caden, our six-year-old daughter Emery, and I were immensely excited to embark upon this journey together. Jennifer and I are both of German heritage, so we thought this would be a nice way for our children to connect with their roots by experiencing life there first-hand.

NO PAIN, NO GAIN
At the same time, I was consumed with a deep sense of fear about my health. Six weeks before we left for Germany, I had undergone back surgery for a herniated disc.

I have had pain up and down my spine since I was fourteen years old as a result of a terrible skiing accident on a family

---

40   Shobhit Seth, "World's Top 10 Software Companies."

vacation in Colorado. In order to continue playing football, basketball, and baseball for my high school teams, I took sixteen Advil nearly every day for the next several years. Many from my hometown of Northbrook, Illinois remember me for sinking two game-winning buzzer beaters in consecutive basketball games my senior year in the latter rounds of the Illinois high school state tournament in 1992.

In overcoming the agony that I had endured in the years leading up to these moments, I learned that the greatest joy in life often emerges from a will to overcome adversity. I still carry this lesson with me today.

In late 2015, my anguish hit a breaking point when I began to feel an excruciating sensation throughout my spine that is difficult to describe in words. There were moments when it felt like my spinal cord was on fire.

Often, I could not sit upright in a chair for more than a few minutes. I spent many nights wandering around the house because the torment prevented me from sleeping. By early 2016, at the age of forty-one, I had reached a point of desperation.

I went to see all kinds of doctors, and I swallowed every pain pill I could get my hands on. One of the specialists I saw finally identified part of the problem. I had a herniated disc at L4–L5 and degeneration in the discs throughout my spine.

This led to the surgery I had in May of 2016, which was successful in clipping the disc that was pressing up against my nerve. Unfortunately, I still had miserable pain following the procedure.

As our plane took off from Washington Dulles airport to Frankfurt on June 15, 2016, I reflected upon the sheer joy I felt to be on this voyage with my family, but also the unrelenting affliction in my back. I was terrified that, just as my condition had prevented me from playing competitive sports after high school, it might now keep me from continuing with the job I loved.

The stakes involved with my spinal problems were much higher now, though, because I had a family to look after. I was concerned about the impact that not being able to work would have on Jordan, Caden, and Emery.

My dad grew up in a small town in Michigan where hard work is a central part of the Midwestern value system.[41] Without the example he set for me growing up, I would not have had the same drive to be successful. I felt that if our kids did not have this same kind of role model, their futures would be adversely impacted. This weighed heavily on me.

So, this was my state of mind as we landed in Frankfurt on June 17, 2016. It was as if I was searching for something that could pull me out of the bottomless pit of chronic pain and resultant anxiety that had overtaken me.

We settled into our place on the Neckar River in Heidelberg, Germany, overlooking the stunning thirteenth-century castle on the hill across from the river which is literally out of a fairy tale.[42] Consuming pain killers each day, I went to the

---

41 Studies Weekly, "The Midwest: People and Characteristics."

42 "10 Fairy Tale Castles To Visit in Germany."

office during the week and we traveled around Germany and neighboring countries on weekends. I was making it through, barely.

AN AUDI FACTORY IN GERMANY

On Saturday, July 16, we decided to try something different. Audi has a museum and an adjacent factory that is open to the public for tours in a town called Neckarsulm.[43] Since engineering is a point of national pride in Germany, Jennifer and I figured that a visit would be a fitting way for our kids to experience this aspect of the culture. We bought tickets online and headed over.

Our factory tour guide Franz greeted us at the entrance with a bellowing German "Hallo." He handed each of us helmets and shields for our eyes to keep us safe, and he explained that there would be absolutely no photos allowed in order to prevent sensitive information from leaking to their competitors BMW and Mercedes. Franz then guided us through a series of highly secure doors.

When we arrived at the factory floor, what did we see? An army of massive robots assembling cars with a level of speed and precision that looked like a scene from a science-fiction movie.

There were just a few humans providing oversight. Franz took us from station to station and explained how Audi had "automated nearly every repetitive task in the production process" of assembling vehicles.

---

43 "Discovery tours."

Franz then pointed to a chart on the wall that depicted how many people were required in the production facility over the past twenty years. Each year showed a drop in the number of humans needed. He said that with improvements in technology, "humans will be eliminated almost entirely from Audi's manufacturing processes." The confidence in his deep voice was striking.

I had spent nearly my entire career in the enterprise software industry, which is focused on automating business processes for global corporations. But, seeing the level of sophistication in these robots, and the clarity with which Franz spoke about the elimination of human workers, really struck me.

Franz then said something I will never forget. He proclaimed that with advances in artificial intelligence and robotic process automation technology, a large percentage of unsuspecting white-collar workers would also see their jobs eradicated. There was no emotion in his voice as he spoke.

Here I was with Jennifer and our three kids on a Saturday afternoon looking to enjoy a nice day together, and Franz was telling us that exponential progress in technology was on the verge of wiping out large swaths of jobs that many thought were not vulnerable to automation.

I looked over at Jordan, Caden, and Emery and I felt my heart sink. I wondered what types of jobs would be left by the time they were ready to seek employment.

Right then and there, at that Audi factory in Neckarsulm, the impact of people losing their jobs became personal to me. I reflected upon the heartbreak my dad felt when he was forced out of work due to Parkinson's disease. I contemplated the fear I had that the pain in my spine would compel me out of my own job. And I worried about what a future full of robots would mean for our kids.

Silently, I thought to myself that it was time to start thinking very differently about how to prepare our kids for a future that would look profoundly different than the past.

THE NORTH STAR

That evening, as I was trying to fall asleep, it dawned on me that something else had recently happened in my life that was significant. In October of 2015, less than a year before our trip to Germany, I had accepted an offer to join the board of directors of NFTE.

Prior to joining SAP, I was an early team member of two highly successful start-ups where I had learned to think like an entrepreneur. And I had seen how valuable it was to apply entrepreneurial thinking inside of a big company like SAP by identifying and capitalizing on opportunities others overlooked. Consequently, I was thrilled to get involved with such a like-minded organization.

Unable to sleep at our place in Heidelberg that night, I opened my computer and went to NFTE's website. When I read through the definitions of the eight domains of the Entrepreneurial Mindset, this time with Audi's robots on my mind, I began to see that this concept had much broader applicability than I had originally envisioned. It occurred to me that this was exactly the mindset that our kids, and all other young people, will need to flourish in the twenty-first century.

On that summer Saturday, a fire began to burn inside of me.

I saw up close how intelligent machines would impact people's livelihoods more pervasively than I had previously grasped. I wanted to be a good father by figuring out how to prepare our kids for this new age ahead. I needed a new mission that was meaningful enough to take my mind off the relentless pain in my spine. And it became clear to me that the Entrepreneurial Mindset was the North Star through which I could bring new purpose to life.

This is the pivotal moment that led me to write this book.

CHAPTER 3

STEPPING BACK IN TIME

———

It is ironic that the impetus for my decision to write this book stems from a visit with my family to a factory run by robots in Germany. I was not aware of this at the time, but our public K-12 educational systems in the U.S. also have their roots in Germany (well, it was the region known as Prussia in the mid-nineteenth century to be more precise).[44]

In 1843, Massachusetts statesman Horace Mann, who later became known as the "Father of the Public School" in the U.S., visited Prussia and brought back with him the Prussian factory model for education. This provided the blueprints for the public K-12 school systems that are still in place today.[45]

An examination of three principles underlying the Prussian paradigm provides useful insights in helping us think about how today's educational systems and pedagogical ideals should be adapted in consideration of the dynamics shaping the twenty-first century.

PRINCIPLE ONE: PRESUMPTION OF KNOWLEDGE SCARCITY VS. KNOWLEDGE ABUNDANCE

The first principle in the Prussian model for early education is the underlying presumption of knowledge scarcity. As a globally recognized voice in education innovation, Tony Wagner summed up the concept of knowledge scarcity vs. knowledge abundance this way:

---

44 Joel Rose, "How to Break Free of Our 19th-Century Factory-Model Education System."

45 Lewis Rincon, "The Development of American Schools."

*The world doesn't care what you know, that's a com-
modity—you can look it up on the internet. What
the world cares about is what you can do with what
you know. Which is a completely different and
brand-new problem in education. We created our
educational systems in an era of knowledge scarcity.
If you wanted to know something you had to go to the
library. We now have a knowledge abundance system, not a knowledge scarcity system. That changes
everything. It changes the purpose of education.*[46]

In this passage, Wagner illustrates a key point about how
intrinsically different the world is today as compared to
the period of Industrialization for which our public K-12
educational systems were originally designed. Information
technology has of course made virtually all publicly available information freely accessible in real time to anyone
with a connected device.

In a world of knowledge scarcity, it made sense to design
curricula around teachers transmitting information to
students. By demonstrating their newfound knowledge
through test taking, students would become more relevant
in an economy that valued this knowledge unto itself. But
in a world that only cares about "what you can do with
what you know," it is critical that we re-consider what
sort of learning methods and educational experiences are
most valuable in readying young people to thrive in the
twenty-first century economy.

---

46   Daniel Araya, *Rethinking US Education Policy: Paradigms of the
     Knowledge Economy*, 116.

PRINCIPLE TWO: EMPHASIS ON CONVERGENT THINKING VS. DIVERGENT THINKING

A second tenet inherent in the Prussian archetype is an emphasis on what renowned psychologist and author J.P. Guilford described as convergent thinking.[47] Generally associated with left-brain aptitudes in popular culture, convergent thinking involves working toward a single "correct" answer. A good example of this sort of deliberation is a multiple-choice exam whereby a student is taught to zero in on the "proper" answer to a question.

Industrialization required a workforce that could precisely handle a repetitive singular process, so getting it "right" every time was essential. Consequently, teaching students to be convergent thinkers was necessary in order to qualify them for the kinds of jobs that the market demanded.

For Guilford, the juxtaposition of convergent thinking is what he calls divergent thinking.[48] More commonly associated with right-brain faculties in popular culture, divergent thinking is a free flow of creative thoughts that generate multiple possible outcomes that are adaptable for a rapidly changing environment. Imagining new ideas without regard to pre-existing structures, developing social intelligence, identifying previously unseen business opportunities, and creating novel ways to solve problems holistically are examples of this type of cognition.

---

47 Olga Razumnikova, "Divergent vs. Convergent Thinking."

48 Sergey Markov, "Joy Paul Guilford – One of the founders of the Psychology of Creativity."

Divergent thinking is not a repetitive process, so job functions that require these uniquely human aptitudes are less likely to be automated. Convergent thinking, in contrast, is precisely where intelligent machines excel. Therefore, young people that learn only to be proficient in this manner and seek employment in fields that don't require much divergent thinking (e.g. truck driving), may quickly find that these occupations are vulnerable to automation.

This is not meant to diminish the importance of convergent thinking or portend that divergent thinking can occur with out acquiring useful information and know-how. The reality is that the two approaches are complimentary and highly synergistic. I am suggesting, however, that our public K-12 educational systems have placed a disproportionate emphasis on convergent thinking, and that its value will be eroded over time by intelligent machines for those that do not also become accomplished divergent thinkers.

Renowned professor and author Sir Ken Robinson explained that a consequence of focusing so heavily on convergent thinking in our K-12 pedagogies is that they are centered on rewarding being right and frowning upon being wrong.[49] Standardized tests, for example, generally measure how well a student can get to the "correct" answer. As a result, students spend an inordinate amount of time "learning to take the test" instead of learning out of curiosity.

For Robinson, the core problem with this second Prussian precept is that it makes students afraid to be wrong, which

---

49   TED, "Do schools kill creativity? | Sir Ken Robinson."

ultimately stifles creativity. "If you're not prepared to be wrong, you'll never come up with anything original," Robinson proclaimed.[50]

The result of this superfluous emphasis on convergent thinking, then, is that "we are educating people out of their creative capacities" and that by the time students finish high school, most have lost their ability to think creatively.[51]

PRINCIPLE THREE: FOCUS ON PREPARATION FOR PROFICIENCY AT REPETITIVE TASKS

A third aim of the Prussian model for schooling was to train workers to be proficient at repetitive tasks required for factory work. Industrialization was becoming a dominant socio-economic force in Prussia and in the U.S. in the nineteenth century. It is no surprise, then, that a solution arose to foster the kind of employees that this transition from an agrarian economy to a manufacturing economy necessitated.

Futurist and author Alvin Toffler captured this point eloquently in his book *Future Shock* as follows:

> *Mass education was the ingenious machine constructed by industrialism to produce the kind of adults it needed. The problem was inordinately complex. How to pre-adapt children for a new world—a world of repetitive indoor toil, smoke, noise, machines, crowded living conditions,*

---

50   Ibid.

51   Ibid.

collective discipline, a world in which time was to be regulated not by the cycle of sun and moon, but by the factory whistle and the clock. The solution was an educational system that, in its very structure, simulated this new world.[52]

As Toffler described in his book, industrial work and the use of assembly lines required a different a kind of mentality than farming. Since factory work tended to subdivide production into many small repetitive tasks with workers often doing only a single task, the market demanded workers with a predisposition for performing the same tasks repeatedly for long hours day after day.[53] In exchange for developing this sort of disposition, employees could expect to hold the same kind of factory job for the entirety of their working lives.

Speaking at the New York City High School Teachers' Association in 1909, statesman Woodrow Wilson explained that the goal of public education in the U.S. was to equip workers for Industrialization. Specifically, he said that public schools existed in order to cultivate students "to perform specific difficult manual tasks."[54] In the eyes of the man that would be elected President of the U.S. four years later, there was little doubt about the objective of public K-12 education in its early years.

Sal Khan, founder of Khan Academy and respected thought leader on modernizing educational systems and pedagogies,

---

52   Alvin Toffler, *Future Shock*, 400.

53   Ibid. 398-427.

54   Woodrow Wilson, "The Meaning of a Liberal Education," 19-31.

offered his insights on this third organizing principle of the Prussian paradigm. "For the time," Khan said, "the Prussian model was forward thinking." He expounded that this was the first time society determined that everyone should be educated, not just the wealthy and culturally elite.[55]

Further, Khan suggested that in bolstering Industrialization, mass education led to the development of the American middle class.[56] In turn, the U.S. economy catapulted into having the largest percentage of world GDP compared to any other nation throughout the twentieth century.[57]

The problem is that we've moved on from the repetitive human labor requirements of Industrialization, but our model for public K-12 education "has been static to the present day," as Khan lamented.[58] While it is undoubtedly the case that curricula, classroom technologies, and culture have progressed over time, this original Prussian design principle of gearing students' mindsets for repetitive tasks remains steadfast within K-12 pedagogies in the U.S.

CONCLUSION

By taking a brief step back in time, we see that our public K-12 educational systems in the U.S. are rooted in the Prussian factory model for schooling which was designed to foster workers for Industrialization. As a result, precepts such as a

---

55 Forbes, "The History of Education."

56 Ibid.

57 Derek Thompson, "The Economic History of the Last 2000 Years Part II."

58 "The History of Education."

presumption of knowledge scarcity vs. knowledge abundance, an emphasis on convergent thinking vs. divergent thinking, and a focus on preparation for proficiency at repetitive tasks still underpin the fundamental nature of how we educate young people.

The twenty-first century economy is, of course, inherently different than the period of Industrialization for which our K-12 pedagogical ideals were originally developed. Next, let's examine some major trends shaping the Future of Work to gain additional perspectives for ascertaining the imperative for change in how we prepare young learners for the modern era.

CHAPTER 4

THE FUTURE OF WORK

—

What will the Future of Work look like?

Let's focus on three trends that are changing both the structure and substance of work in the twenty-first century.

First, job functions involving repetitive tasks or pattern recognition will be automated at an increasingly rapid pace by exponentially advancing intelligent machines. There is strong evidence to suggest that this pervasive technological disruption will lead to new ways of organizing work, and therefore impact the competencies most valued by the marketplace.[59]

Second, digital platforms that match labor supply and demand efficiently are rapidly shifting the essence of employer and employee relationships. This burgeoning Gig Economy, in which independent contractors working remotely take on a growing portion of total economic activity, opens new avenues to earn supplementary income and new opportunities to choose this form of entrepreneurship as a long-term career path. But there are also material downsides involved with this transition to gig work that must be carefully considered.[60]

Third, heightened levels of transparency evoked by the internet and social media have created a growing awareness of the role corporations play in both doing good and causing harm. And crises ranging from the COVID-19 pandemic[61] to climate change have elevated our appreciation for the acute levels of

---

59 "Future of Work | Singularity U Spain Summit 2019."

60 "Sixth annual 'Freelancing in America' study finds that more people than ever see freelancing as a long-term career path."

61 Borge Brende, "COVID-19 Pandemic Shows We Must Reduce Our Blindspot to Risk."

volatility and uncertainty that characterize the twenty-first century.[62] In response, winning companies are recognizing the need for more holistic societal collaboration, and are making changes to no longer be singularly fixated on maximizing profits for shareholders. Instead, they will concentrate more broadly on creating value across their spectrums of stakeholders through purpose-driven Conscious Capitalism.[63]

Taken together, these dynamics are leading to a realignment of the kinds of proficiencies and educational experiences that will be most beneficial moving forward. As such, an analysis of these trends yields important insights for determining how we should adapt our educational systems and pedagogical ideals for the twenty-first century.

TREND ONE: AUTOMATION OF REPETITIVE TASKS AND PATTERN RECOGNITION

Walmart is deploying thousands of robots across its stores to replace workers that unload trucks, scan items, and track inventory among other assignments.[64]

UPS received FAA approval to operate a nationwide fleet of drones that could displace workers that deliver packages across the U.S.[65]

---

62   David Introcaso, "Climate Change Is The Greatest Threat To Human Health in History."

63   Mackey and Sisodia, *Conscious Capitalism*, Chap. 1-2.

64   Nathaniel Mayersohn, "Walmart is doubling down on robot janitors. Here's why."

65   Leslie Josephs, "UPS wins first broad FAA approval for drone delivery."

IBM's Watson saved the life of a woman in Japan by correctly diagnosing her with a rare form of cancer that doctors missed.[66]

Amazon has developed technology to allow consumers to simply buy and go from stores without any human involvement, check-out lines, or even cash.[67]

Accenture eliminated 40,000 internal roles in areas including accounting, procurement, and marketing using automation software that it is now offering to its clients.[68]

We are approaching an inflection point where increasingly rapid improvements in intelligent machines will exceed human abilities to perform job activities consisting of repetitive efforts and pattern recognition. What are the implications of these sweeping technological changes for the Future of Work?

To answer this question, John Hagel, renowned management consultant and Co-Chairman of the Deloitte Center for the Edge in Silicon Valley, suggests that we must first comprehend what drives how work itself is formulated today. For Hagel, the central organizing principle underlying work across all types of enterprises is what he calls "scalable efficiency."[69]

---

66   Jon Fingas, "IBM's Watson AI saved a woman from leukemia."

67   Stephanie Condon, "Amazon offers retailers access to the tech behind Amazon Go."

68   "Accenture to sell software that allowed it to cut 40,000 jobs."

69   "Future of Work | Singularity U Spain Summit 2019."

In effect, today's institutions are governed by a belief that value is maximized by creating efficiencies across an organization at scale. According to Hagel, this assumption has immense impact on how human work is defined and coordinated.[70]

First, work is organized so that every task within an enterprise is tightly defined such that it is handled with maximum efficiency. Second, processes are highly standardized, so they are done in the same productive way across an enterprise. Third, tasks are tightly integrated so all buffers of inefficiency between processes are removed.[71]

Fourth, and perhaps most significantly, work has been organized under the "scalable efficiency" model without the presumption that machine learning, artificial intelligence, and robotic process automation technologies are available to automate repetitive operations and pattern recognition job functions at scale.

The problem with organizing for "scalable efficiency" is that routine tasks and pattern recognition are the core realms of intelligent machines in the twenty-first century. "Machines can do that work so much more efficiently than we humans can," Hagel explained.[72]

He elaborated on one of the hot topics in the Future of Work discourse which involves playing guessing games about what percentage of present-day human job activities will

---

70   Ibid.

71   Ibid.

72   Ibid.

be automated by technology and in what time frame. The McKinsey Global Institute, for example, published a study concluding that "about half of all the activities people are paid to do in the world's workforce could potentially be automated" using currently demonstrated technologies.[73] Hagel argued that this figure could be even higher, and that automation may happen faster than many believe, because of the exponential pace at which intelligent machines are progressing.[74]

Based upon over a decade of research at Deloitte's Center for the Edge, Hagel asserted that the new guiding principle for human work in institutions should become what he calls "scalable learning." This organizational model effectively redefines what human work should be about.[75]

"What work should be," Hagel proclaimed, "is addressing unseen problems and opportunities to create more value." The untapped opportunity, then, is to free humans that are held captive by repetitive routines and pattern recognition operations so they can use their creativity, imagination, and collaborative capacities to solve emerging problems.[76]

To be clear, Hagel does not just refer to innovation labs or research and development departments addressing this type of work. He suggested that *all* workers within an enterprise should shift their focus to identifying and addressing unseen problems in the twenty-first century since *all* repetitive

---

73   Manyika and Chui, "Harnessing automation for a future that works."

74   "Future of Work | Singularity U Spain Summit 2019."

75   Ibid.

76   Ibid.

processes and pattern recognition tasks will ultimately be automated away by intelligent machines.[77]

Another key issue in the Future of Work discourse is the notion that we must re-skill workers when their repetitive assignments or pattern recognition responsibilities are eliminated by technology, all in the name of "scalable efficiency." The dilemma is that once workers are re-skilled to perform the next set of tightly specified operations, it is only a matter of time before these activities are automated away too.[78]

For Hagel, this vicious cycle of human workers getting skilled and re-skilled under increasing pressure to perform each new operation will reach unsustainable levels if the status quo is maintained. There is indeed real justification for fear about massive disruption of jobs, even beyond the displacement resulting from the COVID-19 crisis, if "scalable efficiency" rules as the guiding principle for enterprises in the Future of Work.[79]

As a result, we must re-visit this most basic assumption about what human work should be about in the twenty-first century such that people can escape the unrelenting wave of automation upon us. Instead of applying more human rigor to routine activities and pattern recognition, institutions should cede this ground to intelligent machines, and free people from the monotony of this kind of work.[80]

---

77 Ibid.
78 Ibid.
79 Ibid.
80 Ibid.

Bob Kegan, a developmental psychologist who was the William and Miriam Meehan Research Professor in Adult Learning and Professional Development at Harvard Graduate School of Education, summed it up this way: "Work will increasingly be about adaptive challenges, the ones that artificial intelligence and robots will be less good at meeting."[81] The Future of Work, then, will be about "scalable learning," or bringing people together collaboratively to identify and holistically solve problems at scale.[82]

In short, intelligent machines will handle the boring repetitive tasks and pattern recognition, while we humans are empowered to be more entrepreneurial.

Examples

Let's look at a couple of examples, not from Silicon Valley technology companies, but from traditional industries.[83]

First, a leading tomato processing company in the U.S. made up largely of factory workers processing tomatoes on an assembly line, recently redefined the mission of its team to work together to identify and solve undetected problems within the organization. This is not a group of ex-consultants or advanced degree holders. In fact, many of their team members do not have a college degree.

---

81   Ben Renshaw, *Purpose: The extraordinary benefits of focusing on what matters most,* 85.

82   "Future of Work | Singularity U Spain Summit 2019."

83   Ibid.

In just a brief period, the group realized that a large percentage of their efforts were focused on handling exceptions. By inserting a camera trained to "see" defects in tomatoes as they passed along the line, they were able to re-allocate a substantial percentage of the groups' time to researching new growth opportunities and building stronger relationships with customers.

A second example involves an energy company that manages pipelines across the U.S. This enterprise re-defined the mission of its maintenance workers in the field to not just fix problems after an incident is reported, but to determine how problems could be predicted and prevented before they happen. Additionally, they were coached to look for previously unidentified ways to deliver more value to their various stakeholders.

The team came back with recommendations to use software designed to recognize patterns that was implemented to predict certain kinds of problems before they occurred. By identifying and acting upon this previously unnoticed opportunity to create value, they were able to reduce costs, increase profitability, and improve the environment through more effective containment of spillages.

Implications

Exponentially advancing intelligent machines will drive an unprecedented level of automation across enterprises of all shapes and sizes in the twenty-first century. As a result, the organizing principle for thriving institutions will shift from "scalable efficiency" to "scalable learning."

The implications of these changes on the sorts of aptitudes and pedagogies that will be most advantageous looking forward are six-fold.

First, as work gets re-organized around "scalable learning," jobs will become less about individual tasks and more about project-based collaboration in small, cross-functional teams. Intelligent machines will not be a substitute for complex human collaboration or social intelligence. There will always be demand for these types of skills.

Therefore, providing educational experiences that build communication and collaboration skills through project-based learning is of central importance. Incorporating remote collaboration into these learning methods will take on an even higher level of importance, especially as a result of social distancing protocols brought forth by the COVID-19 pandemic.

Second, successful "scalable learning" organizations will look to hire people that have demonstrated experience with identifying previously undiscovered opportunities and finding innovative solutions to problems. Classroom training that allows students to practice these competencies in cross-disciplinary environments is essential. Ideally, students will establish a portfolio of examples, which they can point to as they seek work experience and consider higher education.

Third, as entrepreneur and investor Bill Joy once said: "No matter who you are, most of the smartest people work for someone else."[84] It is therefore vital that students grasp how to build diverse sets of human relationships that foster collaborative learning as preparation for the Future of Work. Educational environments that encourage students to take initiative in this way will be key.

Fourth, the dramatic shifts resulting from constant technological disruption and global threats will require workers that are highly flexible and adaptable to change. Pedagogies that impart a mindset that is equipped for constant change will be of central importance in enabling students to thrive in the twenty-first century.

Fifth, the most effective "scalable learners" will be those driven by a genuine curiosity for learning. Educational opportunities that allow students to explore topics based on innate passions early and often will be highly beneficial in helping them to identify the best work experience, higher education options, and career paths to suit their areas of interest.

And sixth, knowledge about how technology can be applied is essential in order to identify and develop creative solutions to previously unseen problems in the twenty-first century. Whether it's responding to a crisis like COVID-19, or determining how to process tomatoes more effectively, continuous learning about new scientific and technological advancements is paramount. This highlights the necessity for STEM education early on to establish baseline levels of understanding from which to build upon over time.

---

84 Brook Manville, "How To Get The Smartest People In The World To Work For You."

TREND TWO: THE GIG ECONOMY

"No shifts. No boss. No limits."[85]

This is from a billboard advertisement Uber placed in New York City in 2014. The company's burgeoning ride-hailing platform was made possible by the proliferation of connected mobile devices and sophisticated software algorithms to match supply and demand at a localized level in real-time.

Ultimately, Uber plans to have a fleet of self-driving vehicles to enable their operations. But in the interim, they need human workers to drive passengers from place to place. It would not make sense to hire a workforce of full-time employees, only to eliminate them once self-driving cars become available.

Instead, Uber has sought to bring on independent contractors that could quickly ramp up and down to support driving workloads based on supply and demand. This increasingly widespread use of highly flexible work arrangements through independent contracting and remote work has become known as the Gig Economy.

Author and journalist Sarah Kessler sums up Uber's billboard advertisement this way:

> *These six words embodied the basic pitch with which virtually every gig economy company would lure workers in the years that followed. Freedom from the tyranny of the punch clock, the autocratic*

---

85 Sarah Kessler, *Purpose: The End of the Job and the Future of Work*, 12-13.

boss, the finite wages and limited opportunities of
the 9-5 job. Driving for Uber meant that you were
free. Not only free, but an entrepreneur.[86]

A few decades ago, this pitch may not have been so appealing. For prior generations, there was a well understood career path for achieving the American dream: earn a college degree at a reasonable cost, find a full-time, nine-to-five job with an established organization, and work your way up the hierarchy with promotions every few years.

But the relentless pace of technological change has rendered this formula obsolete. In 1958, companies in the S&P 500 stayed in the index for an average of sixty-one years. By 1980, a study from the research firm Innosight revealed that the average duration on the index had declined to twenty-five years. By 2011, the average tenure had dropped to eighteen years.[87]

If the churn rate continues at this pace, Innosight estimated that the average lifespan of S&P 500 companies will be just twelve years by 2027.[88]

Enterprises have adapted to this rapid change and uncertainty, in part, by minimizing the fixed costs associated with full-time employees. The COVID-19 outbreak has also accelerated remote working for freelancers and full-time workers alike, which will likely lead to a certain level of permanent change

---

86   Ibid.

87   "Creative Destruction Whips through Corporate America."

88   Anthony and Viguerie, "2018 Corporate Longevity Forecast: Creative Destruction is Accelerating."

in this regard.[89] The ease of working remotely using digital communications tools like Zoom, Slack, and Microsoft Teams are further advancing this trend.

Instead of hiring more full-time workers, companies have shifted "non-core" functions to independent contractors that can be easily flexed up or down in response to market dynamics. Part-time workers in the U.S. generally do not receive health care benefits, retirement contributions, vacation time, or basic legal protections which further reduces fixed costs for corporations through transitioning work to independent contractors.

At the same time, digital platforms for Gig Economy workers like Uber, TaskRabbit, DoorDash, Rover, Care.com, and a wide range of others have been created to open entirely new channels for matching freelancers with incremental ways to make money.[90] These gigs have generally been taken on as "side hustles," or work done above and beyond a full-time or other part-time job to bring in additional income.

Do you have a free Saturday afternoon to assemble someone's IKEA furniture? The job is yours through TaskRabbit.

Can you handle a few grocery deliveries after work on Tuesday? The job is yours through DoorDash.

---

89 Maurie Backman, "Could COVID-19 Cause a Permanent Shift to Remote Work?"

90 "Best Gig Economy Apps: 50 Leading Apps to Find Gig Work and Live the Gig Economy Lifestyle."

Are you able to walk a dog Monday night when the owner is out of town? The job is yours through Rover.

Are you free to look after a grandmother that is home alone on Sundays? The job is yours through Care.com.

These dynamics of work being re-allocated to freelancers, coupled with the emergence of digital platforms to facilitate matching labor supply with labor demand and digital communications to enable remote work, have resulted in a massive amount of economic activity occurring through independent contracting. To put this in perspective, 57 million American workers, or thirty-five percent of the workforce, generated over 1 trillion dollars of income through these flexible work arrangements in 2019.[91]

A Tipping Point

In 2019, the Gig Economy hit a tipping point in an even more profound way. For the first time, fully half of all freelancers indicated that they view independent contracting as a long-term career choice rather than a temporary way to make money as a "side hustle."[92]

The trend toward freelancing as a long-term career path is most pronounced among Generation Z (ages eighteen to twenty-two) in which fifty-three percent are actively involved

---

91   "Sixth annual 'Freelancing in America' study finds that more people than ever see freelancing as a long-term career path."

92   Ibid.

in the Gig Economy.[93] Will freelancing become a cornerstone of long-term careers in the Future of Work?

Consider the appeal of being a freelancer for skilled services that can be done remotely from your computer:

- Imagine that you can work from wherever you choose.

- Imagine that you can work whenever you feel most energized.

- Imagine that you can focus your work on only things for which you have a passion.

- Imagine that you don't have to start at the bottom of an organizational hierarchy and work your way up to get ahead.

- Imagine that you can organize your job around your life instead of organizing your life around your job.

This may seem too good to be true, but this is the vision for the Gig Economy espoused by Stephane Kasriel.[94] As the former CEO of UpWork, the world's largest digital platform that connects skilled workers to gigs, he has some unique perspectives on the topic.

Kasriel recently gave an interview to discuss how he sees the Gig Economy evolving in the twenty-first century. During the interview, he was asked what the trend toward gig work means for young people entering the workforce.

---

93 Ibid.

94 Reinvent, "The Future is Freelancing, Says Upwork's CEO."

He responded as follows:

> *Specifically...it means that you are an entrepreneur.*
> *The number of years that you are going to stay at a*
> *company, whether as a freelancer or employee, is a*
> *couple of years. So you'll have ten, fifteen, twenty*
> *careers throughout your life. And you need to plan*
> *for this properly. To me that is entrepreneurship.*[95]

Kasriel went on to explain that students should master from a young age how to think like an entrepreneur, viewing their brain as the product they will ultimately be selling. He said that students should gain experience early on to determine what skills they want to sell, at what price, and how they can uniquely differentiate their skills through skilled labor marketplaces.[96]

With the of rate of digital transformation continuing to accelerate, Kasriel also discussed the importance of instilling the right kind of mindset early and often in young learners. He answered a question about how we should be coaching students to think about the Future of Work as follows:

> *People need to build that (entrepreneurial) mental-*
> *ity. And that is probably one of the biggest failings*
> *of our education system today, is not setting the*
> *right expectations. Yes you can go to college and*
> *that is great...But in practice whatever you have*
> *learned is going to be irrelevant in the next ten*

---

95 Ibid.

96 Ibid.

*years. And you need to have set the expectation
with young people from an early age that it is all
about continuous learning...and not thinking that
when you are twenty-two years old, you've learned
everything you need to learn, and you can just milk
those skills for the rest of your life.*[97]

Kasriel concluded by highlighting the significance of modernizing public policy in the U.S. in consideration of the dramatic shift toward freelancing as a long-term career option in the twenty-first century. Self-employed workers that file taxes with a 1099 form are afforded almost none of the same legal protections as full-time workers filing taxes with a W-2 form. Moreover, as mentioned previously, independent contractors generally do not receive benefits such as health care, vacation time, and retirement contributions.

The American dream of the past has largely been predicated upon people achieving the legal status of a full-time employee or employer. In the Future of Work, the American dream should also be attainable for entrepreneurs that are full-time freelancers in the Gig Economy. Therefore, lawmakers in the U.S. must carefully consider policies that enable entrepreneurs in this growing segment of our economy to thrive in the twenty-first century. The stimulus bill in response to COVID-19 that provided unemployment benefits for gig workers is a sign that awareness of these discrepancies is growing.[98]

---

97 Ibid.

98 Danielle Abril, "Coronavirus stimulus package would dramatically change gig worker benefits. Here's how."

Implications

As a result of digital technologies making it easier for companies to access labor on demand, and with COVID-19 driving increases in remote work more generally, the Gig Economy is in fact reshaping how work gets done in our economy. The days of working nine to five at a single company for an entire career are long gone.

Young people today can expect to have career transitions every few years. They should also prepare to operate as freelancers in the Gig Economy for some parts, if not the entirety, of their working lives. These dynamics have three material implications for what types of learning methods will be most beneficial for students.

First, a premium will be placed on workers that have a high degree of flexibility and adaptability to rapidly changing environments in the Gig Economy. This includes the ability to navigate through both freelancing and full-time working arrangements, as well as through combinations of remote work and on-site job scenarios.

It is often said that in nature, it is not the strongest or the most intelligent who thrive, but rather those that can best manage through change.[99] This sentiment applies to the Gig Economy as well. Educational experiences that simulate real-world scenarios and provide students with opportunities to adapt and respond to rapidly transforming conditions will be exceptionally valuable.

---

99 Shaunta Grimes, "It is not the strongest that survives."

Second, people must develop a future orientation in which they continuously monitor trends and anticipate opportunities to learn new skills that will be in demand in the Gig Economy. Adapting education to include pedagogies designed to instill this capacity to evaluate trends, identify market demands, and create products and services of value is vital to equip students for the twenty-first century.

Third, eighty-nine percent of freelancers surveyed said they wish that their education had better prepared them for the entrepreneurial nature of the Gig Economy.[100] Independent contractors are self-employed free agents in a world that is changing at an increasingly rapid pace.

So, they must adopt the mindset of an entrepreneur to be successful. And, in many ways, the notion of having to adapt one's career every few years—even if working as a full-time employee or employer—requires this same sort of entrepreneurial thinking.

Clearly, the Future of Work necessitates that people learn to think and act like entrepreneurs regardless of the career paths they choose.

TREND THREE: CONSCIOUS CAPITALISM

Can capitalism have a conscience?

Historians will look back on August 19, 2019 as a turning point in the evolution of American capitalism. On that day,

---

100 Upwork, "Freelancing."

the Business Roundtable in Washington, D.C. announced the release of a new Statement of the Purpose of a Corporation which was signed by 181 prominent CEOs. The agreement outlines the CEOs' commitment to lead their companies for the benefit of all stakeholders—customers, employees, suppliers, communities, and shareholders.[101]

This notion of holistically considering value creation across the full range of a company's constituencies, including the environment, is referred to as Conscious Capitalism.[102] It will play a pivotal role in the Future of Work in the twenty-first century, especially as threats like climate change[103] and COVID-19 help us better understand that we must all work together for society to function.[104]

In the decades leading up to the proclamation made by the Business Roundtable in the summer of 2019, the prevailing view in the U.S. of a company's purpose has generally been that its sole objective is to maximize profits for shareholders. Scholars often point to a highly influential 1970 *New York Times* essay authored by Nobel Prize-winning economist Milton Friedman in which he espoused this narrow view of a company's responsibility in society.[105]

---

101 "Business Roundtable Redefines the Purpose of a Corporation to Promote an Economy That Serves All Americans."

102 Mackey and Sisodia, *Conscious Capitalism*, Chap. 2.

103 David Introcaso, "Climate Change Is The Greatest Threat To Human Health in History."

104 Borge Brende, "COVID-19 Pandemic Shows We Must Reduce Our Blindspot to Risk."

105 Milton Friedman, "The Social Responsibility of Business is to Increase its Profits."

In this article, entitled "The Social Responsibility of Business is to Increase its Profits," Friedman went so far as to admonish business leaders that were concerned with constituencies beyond shareholders saying that this was akin to "preaching pure and unadulterated socialism." This essay, and Friedman's body of work more broadly, have shaped the views of business leaders in the U.S. for decades.[106]

Business scholars and economists inserted this single-stakeholder doctrine into their textbooks and related educational content. As a result, effectively everyone who pursued higher education in these arenas in the U.S. thereafter had their thinking influenced by this ideology.[107]

Further, this axiom became codified into various aspects of U.S. corporate law and individual corporate bylaws. Consequently, many boards of directors and corporate officers came to believe that it is their fiduciary duty to serve the singular interest of profit maximization for shareholders.[108]

This ideology is now being challenged, though.

A Transformation is Underway

The radical transparency and ability to rapidly organize brought about by the internet, connected mobile devices, and digital communications has opened the door for a growing movement to hold companies accountable for operating in a socially responsible

---

106 Mackey and Sisodia, *Conscious Capitalism*, Chap. 1.

107 Ibid.

108 Ibid.

manner. This shift toward Conscious Capitalism is being driven by many other entities beyond just the Business Roundtable and the 181 corporations whose CEOs signed its declaration.

For example, another institution leading the charge toward Conscious Capitalism is B Lab. This nonprofit deftly crafted a new type of legal structure called a B Corp which formalizes a company's lawful right to factor in the full plethora of its stakeholders into decision making.[109]

There are now over 2,500 B Corps globally.[110] And more than 50,000 businesses have used the organization's assessment tool to measure and benchmark the impact they are having across their various stakeholders.[111]

Here is an excerpt from B Lab's website that summarizes its charter:

> *Society's most challenging problems cannot be solved by government and nonprofits alone. By harnessing the power of business, B Corps use profits and growth as a means to a greater end: positive impact for their employees, communities, and the environment. The B Corp community works toward reduced inequality, lower levels of poverty, a healthier environment, stronger communities, and the creation of more high-quality jobs with dignity and purpose.[112]*

---

109 "About B Corporations."

110 "How many Certified B Corps are there around the world?"

111 "The B Impact Assessment."

112 "About B Corporations."

Shareholders themselves are also recognizing that society is expecting companies to shift to a more comprehensive approach of creating value across their constituencies through Conscious Capitalism. For instance, Laurence Fink, the Chairman & CEO of BlackRock, which has over $6 trillion in assets under management, called this out in his 2019 annual letter to over 1,000 highly influential CEOs.[113]

"Society is demanding that companies, both public and private, serve a social purpose," Fink wrote. He went on to expound that corporations going forward will be judged not only on financial returns, but also on how they impact society.[114]

Employers and employees too are playing an increasingly significant role in the transformation to Conscious Capitalism. More and more, values such as equality, diversity, and environmental conscientiousness are factoring into decisions about where they choose to work and what opportunities they choose to pursue. For instance, a study done by Accenture and Young Global Leaders found that sixty-one percent of emerging business leaders believe that new business models should be pursued only if profitable growth AND positive societal outcomes can be achieved.[115]

Moreover, a clear and authentic expression of purpose beyond profits is becoming vital for companies to attract and retain talent, particularly pertaining to younger generations. For example, a recent Deloitte study found that

---

113 Larry Fink, "Profit & Purpose."

114 Ibid.

115 "Seeking responsible leadership."

eighty-seven percent of millennial workers believe that "the success of a business should be measured in terms of more than just its financial performance."[116] And research published by Boston Consulting Group found that sixty-seven percent of millennial workers expect their companies to have a higher purpose, and their jobs themselves to have a positive social impact.[117]

In addition, customers are demonstrating a willingness to advocate for Conscious Capitalism, especially among consumers from younger generations. According to a recent Cone Communication study, more than nine out of ten members of the millennial generation would switch brands to one associated with a cause they support.[118]

The survey also indicated that younger generations are disproportionately prepared to take on "personal sacrifices to make an impact on issues they care about."[119] This includes an inclination to pay more for products and services from companies that espouse the values of Conscious Capitalism.[120] In effect, millennial and Gen Z consumers have realized that they can have a material impact on society by banding together and voting with their wallets for companies that adhere to a higher purpose beyond profits.

---

116 "Millennials want business to shift its purpose."

117 Bailey and Bhalla, "Organizing for the Future with Tech, Talent and Purpose."

118 "Cone Communications Millennial CSR Study."

119 Ibid.

120 Ibid.

With CEOs, nonprofits, investors, employees, and customers all exerting their influence on companies to prioritize social responsibility and environmental friendliness alongside profits, expect this transition to Conscious Capitalism to continue in the Future of Work.

Getting Ahead of the Curve

How can companies get ahead of the curve on this movement toward Conscious Capitalism?

In their book, *Conscious Capitalism,* Whole Foods founder John Mackey and Babson College professor Raj Sisodia argue that the first step is for business leaders to recognize that maximizing short-term profits at the expense of other stakeholders is not sustainable.[121]

Here is an excerpt from the book about the consequences of failing to see a higher purpose behind a company's strategy:

> *When business people operate with a low level of consciousness about the purpose and impact of business, they engage in trade-off thinking that creates many harmful, unintended consequences. Such businesses view their purpose as profit maximization and treat all participants in the system as a means to that end. This approach may succeed in creating material prosperity in the short-term, but the resultant price tag of long-term*

---

121 Mackey and Sisodia, *Conscious Capitalism,* chap. 1.

systemic problems is increasingly unacceptable and unaffordable.[122]

For a company to accelerate its evolution to Conscious Capitalism, Mackey and Sisodia declare that there are four interconnected and mutually reinforcing elements required. These four tenets are higher purpose, conscious leadership, stakeholder integration, and conscious culture. Below, I have provided a brief synopsis of each.[123]

Higher purpose, or the reason a company exists beyond maximizing profits, provides a galvanizing force that unites all stakeholders and inspires creativity, imagination, and organizational commitment.[124]

Conscious leaders are individuals that are motivated primarily by serving a company's higher purpose and creating value for all its stakeholders.[125]

Stakeholder integration is the notion that decision-making processes must encompass the full range of a company's stakeholders including customers, employees, suppliers, communities, the environment, and shareholders. Mackey and Sisodia use the phrases "win-win-win-win-win-win" and "win to the 6th power" to describe how value creation is contemplated across these constituencies of a company.[126]

---

122 Ibid.

123 Ibid. chap. 3-18.

124 Ibid. chap. 2-4.

125 Ibid. chap. 5-12.

126 Ibid. chap. 13-14.

Conscious culture flows naturally when *higher purpose* is driven by *conscious leaders* that are fully attuned to *stakeholder integration*. Generally, a *conscious culture* will instill values such as trust, accountability, transparency, commitment, and teamwork.[127]

In the twenty-first century, successful companies will no doubt include those that bring these four precepts of Conscious Capitalism together in an authentic, cohesive, and engaging way alongside their pursuits of maximizing profitability.

Examples of Higher Purpose

Since the centerpiece of Conscious Capitalism is defining a business in terms of its *higher purpose*, I have shared five examples of institutions that have been widely recognized for clearly articulating their charter in this manner:[128]

Disney: To use our imagination to bring happiness to millions.

Johnson & Johnson: To alleviate pain and suffering.

Southwest Airlines: To give people the freedom to fly.

BMW: To enable people to experience the joy of driving.

American Red Cross: Enabling Americans to perform extraordinary acts in the face of emergencies.

---

127 Ibid. chap. 15-18.

128 Mackey and Sisodia, *Conscious Capitalism,* chap. 3.

In these brief illustrations, you can observe how defining the essence of an institution in terms of its higher purpose can have a much more powerful impact across its stakeholders than merely conveying a strategy in terms of maximizing profits.

Implications

Conscious Capitalism will indeed be a major force that impacts the Future of Work in the twenty-first century. The implications of this movement in terms of capabilities and educational experiences that will be most valuable going forward are three-fold.

First, creativity and innovation will take on a more pronounced role in the workplace of the future because these capacities must be applied not only to new products and services, but also to defining and actualizing a higher human purpose for organizations of all sizes. This tendency will open new waves of career advancement opportunities premised on the notion of optimizing purpose alongside profits.

Dr. Bror Saxberg, Vice President of Learning Science for the Chan Zuckerberg Initiative, explained it this way:

> *A lot of work that will continue to be of high value for people is tied to meaning making with other people. This will require a very intentional effort all through the growing-up years and beyond—it is not a thing you pick up the night before you start work.*[129]

---

129 "Getting ready for the future of work."

Therefore, pedagogies that empower students to express and develop their creativity in this manner will be exceptionally rewarding preparation for the twenty-first century.

Second, the elevated importance of customers, employees, and suppliers as key stakeholders will require that critical thinking and holistic problem-solving skills be applied in new ways. Specifically, classroom environments that enable young students to "listen" to customer, employee, and supplier feedback through surveys and publicly available information sources will be especially constructive. Further, students that can master critical thinking and holistic problem-solving skills geared toward improving experiences for these and other key constituencies of an organization will be well prepared to create value in the Future of Work.

Third, the ability to recognize opportunities to create multi-stakeholder value, and the capacity to work toward multi-stakeholder solutions collaboratively with others, will become vitally important in the twenty-first century. For example, team members at Tesla not only design beautiful vehicles for customers, but they also reduce carbon emissions by producing electric vehicles.[130]

And team members at Beyond Meat not only create tasty food for consumers, but they also generate ninety percent less greenhouse gas emissions as compared to producers of ground beef in the U.S.[131] As such, learning methods that cultivate

130 Emily Chasan, "Tesla's First Impact Report Puts Hard Number on CO_2 Emission."

131 Rina Raphael, "Meatless burgers vs. beef: How Beyond Meat's environmental impact stacks up."

students' abilities to collaboratively identify opportunities for multi-stakeholder value creation through project-based learning will be extraordinarily beneficial training for the Future of Work.

CONCLUSION

The Future of Work will be indispensably different than the past in both structure and substance. Dynamics including the automation of repetitive tasks and pattern recognition, the Gig Economy, and Conscious Capitalism are converging to redefine the very essence and purpose of work. This transformation is reconstituting the sorts of aptitudes and learning methods that will be most valuable looking forward.

But to prosper in this novel era upon us, it is imperative that we think beyond just modernizing skill sets that will become obsolete at a pace unlike anything we have witnessed historically. The Future of Work demands that people develop the right kind of mindset so they can flourish in the ever-changing twenty-first century economy.

CHAPTER 5

EIGHT DOMAINS
OF THE MINDSET

——

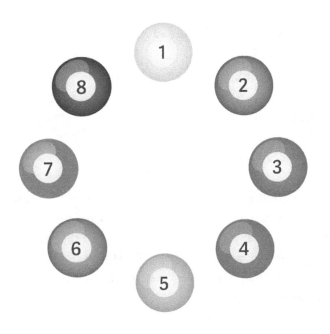

What kind of mindset do people need to thrive in the Future of Work?

The answer is the Entrepreneurial Mindset, or a set of attitudes, behaviors, and skills characterized by eight core domains as follows:[132]

1. Future Orientation

2. Creativity & Innovation

3. Comfort with Risk

4. Communication & Collaboration

5. Flexibility & Adaptability

6. Critical Thinking & Problem Solving

7. Initiative & Self-reliance

8. Opportunity Recognition

This assertion is not meant to suggest that STEM competencies are somehow less important in the twenty-first century, quite the contrary. Few would disagree with the notion that young learners must establish STEM literacies given the central role that these topics play in our modern economy and society.

---

132 "Tools for Life."

But as we explored in Chapter 4, we must also acknowledge that STEM competencies are precisely where exponentially improving intelligent machines shine. Ultimately, human intelligence cannot outpace robots in many of these arenas.

Just ask Lee Sedol, the world's greatest human player of the Chinese game *Go*, which I referenced in the introduction. He recently gave up playing the game since he can no longer compete with intelligent machines from Google.[133]

In order to prepare young people for the twenty-first century economy, we must coach them to prosper with our uniquely human potentialities—the ones that are difficult for robots to automate; the ones that are required to excel in the Gig Economy; and the ones that are ideally suited to create value through purpose-driven Conscious Capitalism. In this way, students can become "robot-proof" for the period ahead.

Before we investigate the eight aspects of the Entrepreneurial Mindset in more depth, consider the journey that led Dr. J.D. LaRock to conclude that fostering this mindset is essential to enable young learners to become "robot-proof."[134]

BECOMING ROBOT-PROOF

As J.D. LaRock sat in the audience of the Harvard Graduate School of Education commencement ceremony in May of

---

133 "Go master quits because AI 'cannot be defeated.'"

134 Joseph E. Aoun, *Robot-Proof: Higher Education in the Age of Artificial Intelligence,* chap. 1.

1997, waiting for his name to be called, he looked up into the clear blue sky and took a deep breath.

His lifelong dream of becoming Dr. J.D. LaRock was just minutes away, and he wanted to capture the fullness of the moment. As the son of New York City public school educators, and a proud graduate of the city's K-12 public school system, education had always been a top priority for him and his family. He thought back to the years of hard work he had poured into arriving at this moment: the long nights in libraries, the pressure-packed tests, and the sacrifice of spending time away from loved ones.

His name was soon called, and he walked across the stage in his black and crimson gown to receive his doctorate. From that point forward, Dr. LaRock knew that his life's work would be about utilizing the power of education to help others achieve their dreams just as he had.

Following a series of high profile positions including serving as senior education policy adviser to the late Senator Ted Kennedy, Dr. LaRock landed a position as chief of staff to Dr. Joseph Aoun, President of Northeastern University in Boston. As a result of their years of experience in education policy research and leadership, Dr. Aoun and Dr. LaRock had both become fascinated with the discourse on how technology was reshaping our world.

Together at Northeastern, the two scholars and a group of researchers set out to develop a framework for how higher education must adapt in the face of this widespread technological disruption. The output of these efforts was a book called *Robot-Proof: Higher Education in the Age of Artificial Intelligence* published in 2017 by MIT Press.

In *Robot-Proof*, Dr. LaRock argued that while literacies in technology and data are of critical importance, simply increasing STEM education is insufficient to formulate students for the twenty-first century. Instead, he contended that we must gear education to evoke a new kind of mindset in students so they can create value in an age where intelligent machines will automate much of the work currently done by humans.[135]

Here is an expert from the book that described this new mindset requirement:

> *A robot-proof model for higher education is not concerned solely with topping off students' minds with high octane facts. Rather, it re-fits their mental engines, calibrating them with a creative mindset and the mental elasticity to invent, discover, or otherwise produce something that society deems valuable.*[136]

This premise that young people must embrace a distinct sort of mindset to prevail in the future has gained widespread support from leaders in business, government, and academia. For example, EY Chairman Emeritus Mark Weinberger proclaimed that when hiring young talent, "We focus on people's mindsets, not just their skill sets."[137] And since mindset often

---

135 Ibid. intro.

136 Ibid.

137 Mark Weinberger, "How new mindsets and diversity are shaping the future of work."

get codified early on in a young person's life, it is insufficient to wait until adulthood to address this most critical requirement for the Future of Work.

Pulitzer Prize-winning author Thomas Friedman emphasized that students must graduate from high school "innovation ready" if they want to be on a path to becoming meaningful contributors in the twenty-first century.[138] And Larry Summers, former U.S. Secretary of Treasury, declared that schools must change to place a premium on "the tasks that machines cannot do: collaboration, creation, and leading."[139]

With this concept of shifting young learners' mindsets fresh in his own mind, Dr. LaRock received a phone call during the summer of 2019 about a CEO opening with NFTE. He was familiar with the organization, dating back to a stint he had done as communications director for New York City public schools two decades prior.

In visiting with teachers and students associated with the nonprofit at the time, he was deeply impressed with their testimonials about the impact that entrepreneurship education had on under-resourced students' lives. In fact, Dr. LaRock wrote extensively about the unique potential of entrepreneurship education in *Robot-Proof*.[140]

As he delved into the institution's transformation that had occurred in the decades since he first learned of its mission,

---

138 Thomas Friedman, "Need a job? Invent It."

139 Lawrence Summers, "Will 2015 be the year of jobless growth?"

140 Aoun, *Robot-Proof*, chap. 3.

Dr. LaRock discovered something extraordinary. He learned that through a collaborative research effort with the Educational Testing Service and EY, the organization had deftly synthesized the elements of the mindset requirements that he had written about in *Robot-Proof*.[141] This compilation of eight core disciplines assembled by the nonprofit was called the Entrepreneurial Mindset.

"This is the best work I have seen on this topic in all of my years as a scholar and leader in the field of education," Dr. LaRock said. He went on to explain how the organization had developed a groundbreaking measurement system for quantifying each component of the mindset, along with a revamped curriculum designed to instill the mindset in its students. Dr. LaRock concluded that collectively, these components provided an exceptional foundation upon which to build.

As CEO of a public-private partnership reporting to the Governor of Massachusetts and responsible for driving the innovation agenda for K-12 schools across the state, Dr. LaRock was not seeking a new position when he got that call in the summer of 2019. At the same time, it was clear NFTE could provide a national and global platform through which he could influence the trajectories of students' lives on a broader scale. When the offer came in, he knew it was the right fit, and he accepted.

Dr. LaRock's mission as the CEO of NFTE is, of course, to help students become "robot-proof" for the twenty-first century.

---

141 "NFTE Releases New Research on Measuring Entrepreneurial Thinking in Young People."

THE EIGHT DOMAINS

As thought leaders like Dr. LaRock and many others coalesce around the viewpoint that we must help young learners build a distinct mindset in consideration of the Future of Work, it is important that we clearly define the eight core domains that constitute this ethos.

Each aspect of the Entrepreneurial Mindset has something in common: they all require a high degree of uniquely human right-brain cognition, the sort of non-repetitive thought patterns that are difficult for intelligent machines to emulate. Young people who become decidedly proficient in these eight realms, in addition to developing robust STEM literacies, will be well positioned to become "robot-proof" for the age upon us.

Let's examine each of these eight domains below:[142]

Future Orientation
An optimistic disposition with a focus on obtaining the skills and knowledge required to transition into a career.

Creativity & Innovation
The ability to think of ideas and create solutions to problems without clearly defined structures.

Comfort with Risk
The capacity to move forward with a decision despite inevitable uncertainty and challenges.

Communication & Collaboration
The ability to clearly express ideas to an intended audience, including persuading others to work towards a common goal.

---

142 "Tools for Life."

Flexibility & Adaptability

The ability and willingness to change actions and plans to overcome present and future challenges.

Critical Thinking & Problem Solving

The capacity to apply higher-level, process-oriented thinking, consider an issue from a range of possible perspectives, and use that reasoning to make decisions.

Initiative & Self-Reliance

The power to take ownership of a project without input or guidance and work through obstacles independently.

Opportunity Recognition

The practice of seeing and experiencing problems as opportunities to create solutions.

1) Future Orientation

A future orientation is an optimistic disposition with a focus on obtaining the skills and knowledge required to transition into a career.

People with a future orientation have a high level of curiosity and view learning as a lifelong pursuit. They continuously explore trends across a broad range of technological, societal, economic, and environmental factors and formulate hypotheses that forecast how these dynamics may impact the status quo. And they maintain a positive outlook about getting to a better future, irrespective of challenges that may arise.

Microsoft provides a good illustration of how important it is to develop a future orientation in the twenty-first century, having put this concept at the center of its recently revamped company culture. In orchestrating one of the great corporate turnarounds of the last decade, Microsoft CEO Satya Nadella became convinced that the company must move to a "learn it all" culture in place of its previous "know it all" culture. For Nadella, a "learn it all" culture is one where ALL employees make new learning, experimentation, and exploration of future trends a top priority.[143]

In previous eras, the pace of change was much slower. Therefore, knowing a lot about the status quo was enough to sustain market leadership in many cases.

But in an age of exponential change, everyone must adapt themselves to become a future-oriented continuous learner. In this way, organizations can respond quickly enough to market dynamics and threats that may come from completely unrelated industries or unanticipated sources.

As a case in point, who would have ever imagined that an online bookstore would enter the market for corporate computing and end up dominating entire segments of this seemingly unrelated industry? This is exactly what happened when Amazon Web Services sprung out of Amazon's core online retail business.

By evolving into its new "learn it all" culture with a future orientation at its core, Microsoft was able to identify this threat and respond just in time to prevent Amazon from running away with the massive new market opportunity for cloud computing.[144]

---

143 Terence Mauri, "Want To Think Like Satya Nadella? Follow 3 Simple Rules."

144 Sergei Klebnikov, "Microsoft Is Winning The 'Cloud War' Against Amazon: Report."

2) Creativity & Innovation

Creativity and innovation are the ability to think of ideas and create solutions to problems without clearly defined structures.

Individuals who are creative and innovative have a demonstrated ability to imagine the art of the possible, while also considering factors required to turn a new vision into reality. They are skilled at asking questions, listening, and synthesizing information from a wide range of sources to conceptualize and generate novel ideas. And they can then translate these new ideas into solutions that create tangible value.

There is widespread evidence behind the growing importance of creativity and innovation in the twenty-first century. For example, a survey by IBM asked 1,500 business leaders around the globe to name the top quality they look for in leaders.

The number one answer? Creativity.[145]

In another survey from PWC, creativity and innovation were identified as the top two skills that 77 percent of CEOs are seeking in hiring new talent.[146] Furthermore, LinkedIn found that creativity was the single most in demand soft skill in 2019, based on data gathered from its users and over twenty million job postings on its site.[147] And research from the World Economic Forum placed creativity in the top three

---

145 "IBM 2010 Global CEO Study: Creativity Selected as Most Crucial Factor for Future Success."

146 "The talent challenge: Harnessing the power of human skills in the machine age."

147 Bruce Anderson, "The Most In-Demand Hard and Soft Skills of 2020."

skills that are most in demand this year from employers around the world.[148]

Creative and innovative thinkers will clearly become indispensable in the Future of Work. As perhaps the most difficult domain within the Entrepreneurial Mindset for intelligent machines to replicate, creativity and innovation are unsurprisingly among the most important potentialities for people to build in order to become "robot-proof."

3) Comfort with Risk

Comfort with risk is the capacity to move forward with a decision despite inevitable uncertainty and challenges.

Those who are comfortable with risk have a practiced aptitude to assess risk and reward trade-offs. They possess the confidence to navigate through nebulous and unpredictable environments. And they have the sensibility to continuously evaluate a diverse array of risk factors, while dynamically formulating strategies to respond to these risks.

It is often said that the Future of Work will be characterized by unusually high levels of Volatility, Uncertainty, Complexity, and Ambiguity (VUCA), largely due to exponentially advancing technologies.[149] Global crises such as COVID-19[150] and

---

148 Alex Gray, "The 10 skills you need to thrive in the Fourth Industrial Revolution."

149 Sunnie Giles, "How VUCA Is Reshaping The Business Environment, And What It Means For Innovation."

150 Borge Brende, "COVID-19 Pandemic Shows We Must Reduce Our Blindspot to Risk."

climate change add even higher levels of unpredictability.[151] As I referenced in Chapter 4, in 1958 the average lifespan of a company in the S&P 500 index was sixty-one years.[152] By 2027, it is estimated that this lifespan will decrease to just twelve years.[153]

Which companies have the highest risk of folding? Which industries will die off, and what new industries will emerge? Which job functions are most likely to be automated by intelligent machines?

People must master the ability to be comfortable in these sorts of high-risk, rapidly changing, and ambiguous environments because they are ever-present in the twenty-first century.

4) Communication & Collaboration

Communication and collaboration are the ability to clearly express ideas to an intended audience, including persuading others to work toward a common goal.

Individuals who can communicate and collaborate effectively are able to develop clear objectives, deliver persuasive arguments, speak proficiently in public, inspire others to action, and lead diverse groups of people. They have a high degree of empathy, cultural awareness, and social intelligence in their interactions with others. And they are adroit in their use of all

---

151   David Introcaso, "Climate Change Is The Greatest Threat To Human Health in History."

152   Creative Destruction Whips through Corporate America."

153   Anthony and Viguerie, "2018 Corporate Longevity Forecast: Creative Destruction is Accelerating."

forms of collaboration, ranging from in person meetings and video conferences to social media and digital communications.

To state this discipline more concisely, young people must learn how to interact with other people. It sounds so simple, doesn't it?

But it has become distressingly obvious that social media, mobile devices, virtual reality gaming, and other technologies have reduced social interactions for young people. This in turn stunts the development of emotional intelligence as they mature into adults. Moreover, the adoption of social distancing as a result of the COVID-19 outbreak is likely to exacerbate this trend.[154]

As human beings, our mental and emotional well-being is inextricably linked to the quality of the human relationships we develop and maintain over time. I have not yet come across a lot of research indicating that robots can be a substitute for meaningful human to human relationships. This has very positive implications for people who proactively work to boost their communication and collaboration skills.

Award-winning *Fortune* columnist and author Geoffrey Colvin described these implications in his book *Humans are Underrated* as follows:

> As technology takes over more of our work while simultaneously changing us and the way we relate to one another, the people who master the human

---

154 "How COVID-19 Could Affect Kids' Long-Term Social Development."

abilities that are fading all around us will be the most valuable people in our world.[155]

Similarly, acclaimed data and policy analyst from research firm Acumen, LLC Frank Elavsky explained:

> *The most important skills to have in life are gained through interpersonal experiences...[that] stimulate real compassion, empathy, vulnerability and social-emotional intelligence. These skills are imperative to focus on, as the future is in danger of losing these skill sets from the workforce.*[156]

Without question, building strong communication and collaboration skills is an essential element to equip young learners for the future.

5) Flexibility & Adaptability

Flexibility and adaptability are the ability and willingness to change actions and plans to overcome present and future challenges.

People who are flexible and adaptable have a high degree of persistence and grit, which enables them to operate effectively in rapidly changing and volatile environments. They are open to new ideas and able to cope when objectives shift unexpectedly or when things don't go as planned. And they can bounce back quickly with alternative plans when obstacles thwart their efforts to attain goals.

---

155 Geoffrey Colvin, *Humans are Underrated: What High Achievers Know That Brilliant Machines Never Will*, 67.

156 Rainie and Anderson, "The Future of Jobs and Jobs Training."

Consider the following characterization of the Future of Work in *Wired Magazine* as authored by renowned digital analyst and researcher Brian Solis:

> *This is a time of digital Darwinism—an era where technology and society are evolving faster than businesses can naturally adapt. This sets the stage for a new era of leadership, a new generation of business models, charging behind a mantra of "adapt or die."*[157]

English biologist Charles Darwin is well known for theorizing that it is neither the strongest nor most intelligent that survive in the natural world, but rather the most adaptable to change.[158] Given the nature of the exponential technological change in the modern era, this theory may in fact be equally applicable in the twenty-first century.

And with COVID-19 leading to more remote work, an even higher level of adaptability is necessary—especially pertaining to developing personal networks that have historically been built through in-person contact. Those who embrace a mentality of flexibility and adaptability will certainly become more "robot-proof" than those that are incapable or unwilling to accept constant change as the new normal.

Increasingly, thought leaders support the notion that flexibility and adaptability are a new sort of mindset qualification for the

---

157 Brian Solis, "Digital Darwinism: How Disruptive Technology Is Changing Business For Good."

158 "It Is Not the Strongest of the Species that Survives But the Most Adaptable to Change."

twenty-first century. Cecile Alper-Leroux, VP of Human Capital Management innovation at Ultimate Software, framed it this way:

> *To survive rapid technological shifts, we must build adaptability and resilience directly into our work forces. Many organizations have paid lip service to shifting recruitment toward critical professional skills like self-awareness and empathy, but the reality is too many business leaders and recruiters are still prioritizing technical skills that may be obsolete in a few years.[159]*

Others have called out the specific need for educational experiences that build this kind of mentality. Dr. Srini Pillay, assistant professor at Harvard Medical School, summed it up nicely stating, "If you say to people, 'You need to adapt,' but you don't help them learn how to build a change-oriented mindset, it doesn't really help."[160]

This sentiment highlights the need to identify and implement pedagogies that are designed to assist young people in establishing this sort of "change-oriented mindset."

6) Critical Thinking & Problem Solving

Critical thinking and problem solving are the capacity to apply high level, process-oriented thinking, consider an issue

---

159 Marcel Schwantes, "3 Big Future of Work Trends Every Leader Should Know About."

160 "Getting ready for the future of work."

from a range of possible perspectives, and use that reasoning to make decisions.

Those with well-developed critical thinking and problem-solving skills seek to balance the application of data and technology holistically, with a degree of human intuition and judgement when making important determinations. They can think on their feet, assess problems interactively, and work toward solutions. In addition, they can develop well thought out solutions either as part of a team or independently.

In assessing the top skills required for the Future of Work, the World Economic Forum placed problem solving and critical thinking as number one and number two on their list, respectively.[161] There is little disagreement about the vital nature of these competencies for a future characterized by VUCA.

Of the eight domains, however, critical thinking and problem solving are perhaps most closely linked to the sort of left-brain convergent thinking that may be more vulnerable to automation. But there is a key distinction between this realm and critical thinking and problem solving as it pertains to handling repetitive processes or pattern recognition.

Here, we are referring to identifying previously unseen problems and using holistic thought processes to evaluate alternatives with contextual understanding to ultimately arrive

---

161 Alex Gray, "The 10 skills you need to thrive in the Fourth Industrial Revolution."

at conclusions that solve problems. Intelligent machines will continue to advance in their ability to assess, diagnose, recognize patterns, and make predictions.

But there will always be a place in the Future of Work to apply holistic human judgement, cultural awareness, ethical guidance, strategic insight, and broader context to solving problems.

7) Initiative & Self-reliance

Initiative and self-reliance are the power to take ownership of a project without input or guidance and work through obstacles independently.

Individuals who demonstrate initiative and self-reliance are proactive about identifying new ways to create value and have the grit to see projects through. They can determine what needs to be learned, manage time effectively, and generate positive outcomes with little oversight. They are also very self-aware and understand how to align organizational and project-specific objectives to their own sense of purpose in order to sustain the highest level of performance throughout an initiative's life cycle.

Consider how the Gig Economy and the trend toward having a "new" career every two to three years due to the increased pace of change impacts the mindset requirements for young people. In previous times, one could ride out an extensive portion of their working lives based upon a specific learned skill set or through networking within a specific company.

In a *New York Times* article entitled "Need a job? Invent It," Pulitzer Prize-winning author Thomas Friedman summed it up this way:

> *My generation had it easy. We got to "find" a job. But, more than ever, our kids will have to "invent" a job. Sure, the lucky ones will find their first job, but, given the pace of change today, even they will have to reinvent, re-engineer and re-imagine that job much more often than their parents if they want to advance in it.*[162]

In the Future of Work, initiative and self-reliance take on a new level of importance because one must simultaneously deliver on the project at hand while learning new skills and hunting for the next gig or career move. Those that consistently take this initiative to prepare themselves to move fluidly from one opportunity to the next will be well positioned to become "robot-proof" for the twenty-first century.

Those that do not establish the ability to think and act like an entrepreneur in this way will be far more susceptible to automation.

8) Opportunity Recognition

Opportunity recognition is the practice of seeing and experiencing problems as opportunities to create solutions.

People with a keen ability to recognize opportunities can synthesize information in such a way that they see new approaches

---

162 Thomas Friedman, "Need a job? Invent It."

or market niches that others overlook. People that become highly proficient in this domain, coupled with advanced STEM literacies, will have a vast array of opportunities to identify in applying rapidly progressing technologies to solve problems. And those that master the techniques required to capitalize on these opportunities will most certainly be highly rewarded as "robot-proof" value creators.

There is one important macro opportunity that I want to recognize here, which I referenced in the previous chapter. This is the notion that winning companies in the Future of Work will embrace a multi-stakeholder, purpose-driven mission inherent in Conscious Capitalism.[163]

As we collectively grapple with sweeping challenges that impact all aspects of our future such as pandemics like COVID-19, climate change, poverty, and other Strategic Development Goals (SDGs) set forth by the United Nations General Assembly in 2015,[164] it is essential that we seize this opportunity to move to a more inclusive form of capitalism. Companies that align their missions to a higher purpose that positively impacts their full portfolio of stakeholders—and young people that strive to be purpose-driven in this same manner—will be well-positioned to flourish in the Future of Work.

CONCLUSION

The eight domains of the Entrepreneurial Mindset are indeed essential for people to thrive in the twenty-first century

---

163 Mackey and Sisodia, *Conscious Capitalism*, chap. 2-4.

164 "Sustainable Development Goals."

economy. The Future of Work necessitates that we identify ways to foster this ethos in students for them to become "robot-proof."

In Chapter 7, we'll explore a curriculum that is designed precisely with the aim of helping young learners build these domains. But as our school systems evaluate the merits of bringing project-based entrepreneurship education into the classroom, a question invariably arises.

How do we measure the Entrepreneurial Mindset and monitor it for continuous improvement? This is the topic we'll tackle next, in Chapter 6.

CHAPTER 6

MEASURING THE MINDSET

A gut feeling. An instinct. An intuition.

These are the words Dr. Thomas Gold used to describe his state of mind as he sat pensively alone at the kitchen table in his apartment in New York City.

It was a lively summer Saturday, the kind of day when most people are outside enjoying the weather. Joggers were out jogging. Bikers were out biking. Basketball courts and tennis courts were packed. The New York Yankees had a standing room only crowd at their home game.

But Dr. Gold, a Mets fan, was oblivious to anything that was going on outside of his own brain. His mind was racing toward a big idea, and nothing was going to stop him from bringing this idea to fruition.

Dr. Gold was laser focused on survey results coming in from employers across the world showing that so-called "soft skills" like creativity, communication, collaboration, and initiative were increasingly topping the list of competencies that were most in demand. The problem was that New York City public schools—the focal point for his research—lacked a clear methodology to test or teach these skills to students.

It was viewed by some within New York City public policy circles that these types of capacities could not be measured and, therefore, were not worth pursuing in K-12 curricula. Dr. Gold believed that the exact opposite was true, and was determined to find a solution to upend the status quo.

THE ENTREPRENEURIAL MINDSET INDEX[165] (EMI) IS BORN

To those who have experienced project-based entrepreneurship education up close, the impact on students is obvious. Classroom engagement is high because students choose their own topics of interest.

Curiosity thrives. Passions are discovered and pursued instead of ignored. Business plans are created from scratch. New skills are developed. Confident presentations are made by students who were once terrified of public speaking.

But how should achievement be measured in teaching entrepreneurship when there are no "correct" answers as there are with more traditional academic subject matter?

This is a question that educators, administrators, and policy makers like Dr. Gold have grappled with regarding "non-academic" courses for years.[166] Some go so far as to suggest that if outcomes can't be measured, then the subject simply isn't worthy of being taught at all in K-12 schools.

But given the overwhelming evidence that the ability to think and act like an entrepreneur is fundamental to achieving success in the twenty-first century, it was only a matter of time before a measurement mechanism was developed.

---

165 Gold and Rodriguez, "Measuring Entrepreneurial Mindset In Youth: Learnings From NFTE's Entrepreneurial Mindset Index."

166 Dian Schaffhauser, "Measuring Academic and Nonacademic Skills Equally Important."

Raised in a household with an academic father and a mother who studied psychology, Dr. Gold grew up surrounded by people who believed that any idea worth pursuing must be backed up by hard data. "We would have arguments about politics at our dinner table nearly every night. I was never criticized for having an opinion. But, making a point without supporting it with facts was taboo in the Gold household," he said. Dr. Gold joked that using data to support arguments may as well have been written into his DNA.

This notion of data-driven thinking was reinforced throughout his own education which culminated with the completion of his PhD in political science at the New School for Social Research in New York City. And in his career, Dr. Gold had completed countless projects focused on bringing a rigorous analytical lens to topics such as equity and access in education. His work enabled New York City public schools to make more informed decisions on these and other important policy matters.

Dr. Gold spent nearly a decade leading K-12 education policy research and evaluation for New York City public schools under Chancellor Joel Klein and Mayor Michael Bloomberg. He would later go on to work for renowned professor Dr. James Kemple to help him build the Research Alliance for New York City Schools at NYU.

Dr. Gold loved his work. But, this vexing issue of how to grapple with teaching "soft skills" to students kept appearing in his research, and it was giving him pause.

Everyone agreed with the data coming in from employers regarding the increasing importance of these skills,[167] but nobody had any answers for what to do about it. Dr. Gold struggled to identify an approach to convince his colleagues that New York City (and other places for that matter) was failing its students by not equipping them with an entire category of skills that employers obviously wanted. He grew increasingly frustrated that the system seemed content to accept the situation as it was.

On that beautiful Saturday in the summer of 2013 in New York City as he sat alone at the kitchen table in his apartment, Dr. Gold became obsessed with finding a solution to this problem. On a whim, he decided to open the LinkedIn app on his phone. He wanted to determine who else might be doing research on measuring and teaching "soft skills."

Unexpectedly, a job posting caught his attention. The position was for a VP of Research role that would be tasked with studying and measuring at the middle and high school level the same sorts of skills for which New York City public schools had no solution. The organization looking to make the hire was NFTE, which Dr. Gold was only vaguely familiar with at the time.

In examining the nonprofit's work, Dr. Gold began to theorize that perhaps project-based entrepreneurship education was the best vehicle through which these "non-academic" competencies could be taught and measured in young people.

---

167 Bruce Anderson, "The Most In-Demand Hard and Soft Skills of 2020."

The more research he did, the more his theory seemed to ring true. As a result, he decided to go ahead and apply for the position.

As he made his way through the interview process, Dr. Gold got into lengthy discussions with NFTE's leadership team about the vision for the organization and the research underway to distill the Entrepreneurial Mindset into eight core domains. He could see that these aptitudes were very closely aligned with the "soft skills" employers were demanding.

During one of these conversations, Dr. Gold had an epiphany. "It occurred to me that if we took these eight domains as a given, I could then focus my research and evaluation expertise on creating a measurement system to quantify a student's proficiency for each one," Gold noted. It was a difficult decision to leave behind the work he was doing at NYU, but the opportunity to bring a ground-breaking learning method to students that would prepare them for the sweeping changes ahead was too great to pass up.

Dr. Gold decided to accept the position and pour his energy into solving a problem that many seemed to think was unsolvable. Just as the SAT and other standardized tests were developed to measure certain academic skills and preparedness for college, the new system would provide a rigorous method to measure and improve the eight domains of the Entrepreneurial Mindset and preparedness for the Future of Work.

It would be called the Entrepreneurial Mindset Index (EMI).[168]

---

168 Gold and Rodriguez, "Measuring Entrepreneurial Mindset."

EMI PRINCIPLES

There were three guiding principles that Dr. Gold used in creating the EMI. First, he and his team decided to partner on the research effort with the Educational Testing Service (ETS), which develops and administers over 50 million tests in 180 countries. EY was also brought in as a strategic partner to help fund the EMI research effort.

The team wanted to capture lessons learned from these market leaders in the industry. ETS had been working extensively on similar innovative approaches to assessing "non-academic" capacities like persistence, motivation, and the ability to work with others. And EY had done extensive consulting work in providing services to entrepreneurs and studying the factors that determined their success.

"We found that ETS and EY were keenly interested in helping us create a psychometrically sound way to measure the Entrepreneurial Mindset," Dr. Gold said.[169] He went on to explain that there was general agreement among the participants that traditional cognitive assessments provide a relatively narrow view of a student's intelligence, capacities, and skills.

Further, the collaborative research effort helped the team realize that universities too were looking for students with demonstrated proficiencies in the eight domains of the Entrepreneurial Mindset. And like K-12 schools, they also were struggling with the notion of how to quantify these sorts of capabilities.

---

169 Ibid.

Second, Dr. Gold would draw on techniques stemming from different disciplines. These would include entrepreneurship education, item response theory, and various areas of psychology including Industrial and Organization (I/O), a rapidly growing field focused on testing human behavior in the workplace.[170] Since the goal of the Entrepreneurial Mindset was to equip students for the Future of Work, he felt factoring in research from across these arenas was crucial.

The team's assessment of the tools and methods used in these fields led them to conclude that Likert scale questions,[171] in which answers span from strongly agree to strongly disagree, were the most basic way to measure the mindset realms. However, they wanted to introduce more innovative approaches to measurement that were also emerging. Thus, the team determined that situational judgement tests should also be incorporated into the EMI, given their utility for scenarios where decision making is involved.[172]

In addition, other studies have identified the importance of measuring students' internal locus of control, or the extent to which they believe they are empowered from within to achieve their goals. Psychological research has found that people with a higher internal locus of control tend to be higher achievers in school and in the workplace.[173] As such, the team agreed that it was important to capture this concept within the EMI as well.

---

170 "Industrial and Organizational Psychology."

171 "Learn when and how to use Likert scale questions."

172 "Situational judgement tests."

173 Richard Joelson, "Locus of control."

Third, Dr. Gold wanted the team to administer testing to pilot groups over multiple school years so they could assess results before the tool was rolled out to larger student populations. This would enable them to establish statistical significance and reliability for changes that occurred in EMI test results measured before vs. after the completion of portions of the project-based entrepreneurship curriculum. It would also allow them to incorporate feedback from teachers and students from pilot engagements so that adjustments could be made accordingly.

Over 10,000 EMI test results were accumulated during the pilot phase. The evidence became clear that the EMI can, in fact, measure students' mindsets across the eight core domains.[174]

This information could then be used by teachers and students to personalize the learning experience throughout the curriculum, in order to accentuate strengths and improve upon weaknesses. As a result, the EMI is now being implemented across other classrooms in order to facilitate these enhancements to students' mindsets.

Dr. Gold is immensely proud of achieving something that many said was impossible. Now, when he sits down for dinner with his family, he has real data to substantiate the gut feeling he had that "soft skills" can indeed be taught, measured, and improved upon in young learners.

But instead of using generic terms like "soft skills," he now prefers to be more precise in referring to the eight domains

---

174 Gold and Rodriguez, "Measuring Entrepreneurial Mindset."

of the Entrepreneurial Mindset as what employers are really looking for in hiring talent for the twenty-first century.

ENABLING THE EMI WITH SOFTWARE

Sophia Rodriguez is the kind of person that doesn't just talk about ideas; she makes them happen. She first made her mark as a high school student in Miami where she organized a walk-a-thon to raise money for school supplies for kids in the small town in India where she was born.

Having immigrated to the U.S. at the age of nine, Rodriguez had always wanted to re-visit her hometown. At age sixteen, upon returning to India on a family trip, she was dismayed to see that schools lacked basic supplies needed for students to learn.

Rodriguez's fundraising effort was so inspiring that it has continued as an annual event in Miami for over a decade now to finance school supplies for children all over the world. This initiative was just the beginning of her penchant to turn great ideas into reality.

After earning degrees from NYU in social entrepreneurship and public policy, Rodriguez spent five years as the director for the undergraduate business dean of NYU focused on cutting edge curriculum in areas including entrepreneurship and data science.

She earned high praise at the university not just for her ideas, but for successfully implementing these enhancements in courses at the school. During her tenure at NYU, Rodriguez also began to develop a keen interest in K-12 education.

"While my colleagues at other universities and I were rapidly adapting our curriculum and programs for the Future of Work, I did not find this same sense of urgency in K-12," Rodriguez observed. "I could see an increased focus on STEM, but I feared that our young students were being left behind when it came to other abilities that employers are increasingly demanding."

Rodriguez cited research she led at NYU that showed rising employer demand for competencies such as creativity, innovation, the ability to recognize opportunities, and adaptability to work collaboratively with diverse groups of people to holistically solve problems. When a recruiter contacted Rodriguez about a position to apply her skills at the middle and high school level for NFTE, she jumped at the opportunity.

She was attracted to the organization in part because of its deep roots in advanced research. For example, the nonprofit published results of a pioneering joint research effort with the Harvard School of Education in the early 2000s. The study concluded that students in Boston Public Schools who were completing entrepreneurship courses had a greater interest in career development and attending college because they were able to connect what they were learning to the "real world."[175]

---

175 "Expanded Explorations Into The Psychology of Entrepreneurship: Findings From The 2001-2002 Study of NFTE in Two Boston Public High Schools."

"In NFTE, I saw an organization with a track record of bringing the kind of innovation that is so badly needed in early education," Rodriguez explained. Joining the nonprofit in February of 2017, she immediately joined forces with Dr. Gold on the EMI initiative.

Rodriquez believed in the initiative's revolutionary potential, and she wanted to be part of the team that would make it happen. Her first assignment was to identify and implement a technology platform upon which the EMI could be implemented.

Rodriquez grouped the work around the EMI into a set of technology requirements that were then submitted to a range of software providers through an RFP process. In addition to meeting their defined functional requirements, she documented in the RFP that flexibility, usability, proven deployments for similar projects, and customer references would also be key criteria for consideration.

In the end, only one software company earned perfect scores across each criterion outlined in the RFP. The winner was a company called Qualtrics based in Provo, Utah.

The company's name is a play on the words "qualitative" and "analytics," suggesting the ability to measure concepts that are difficult to measure. This of course fits quite nicely with the idea behind the EMI.

Today, Qualtrics is the global market leader in a category of enterprise software called Experience Management, or XM.[176]

---

176   "Qualtrics Ranked #1 Enterprise Leader for Customer Experience and Employee Experience in Industry-Leading Product Ranking."

The company originally got its start as a research platform for academia.[177]

In fact, over 11,000 institutions utilize the Qualtrics research platform, including 99 of the top 100 business schools in the world.[178] Rodriquez had used the software in her research efforts at NYU, so that gave her an even higher level of confidence that the company could deliver on the teams' vision for the EMI.

Rodriquez proceeded with her colleagues and the team from Qualtrics to implement the EMI, where they administered the pilot phase to over 10,000 students. Coupling the EMI methodology with the Qualtrics platform turned out to be a winning combination. The pilot was a huge success, and as mentioned, the tool is now being rolled out more broadly.

In bringing the EMI to life through Qualtrics, Rodriquez proved once again that her reputation for turning great ideas into reality is well deserved.

EMI IN THE CLASSROOM

Imagine a high school teacher of twenty-five years transforming from a "sage on stage" to a "guide on the side." This is how 2019 NFTE Model Teacher of the Year award winner[179] Sandra Cruz described her journey in switching gears from teaching

---

177 "Qualtrics Dominates Academic Survey Research."

178 "Trusted by over 11,000 of the world's leading brands and 99 of the top 100 business schools."

179 "Eight Educators Advance to Final Round of National Competition in NFTE Model Teacher Challenge."

technical skills such as graphic design and web development to becoming an educator of project-based entrepreneurship.

Cruz was drawn to the challenge because she wanted to have an impact on her students beyond just teaching them technical skills. Keenly aware that her students would enter a future requiring them to adapt their skills every few years, Cruz wanted to shape her students' ethos more broadly to equip them. Instilling the Entrepreneurial Mindset is exactly what Cruz has been doing with her students by using the EMI in her classroom at Thomas A. Edison Career and Technical Education High School in Queens, New York.

Growing up in Queens, Cruz was the fourth of six children that her parents had together upon immigrating from the Dominican Republic. "Earning $11,000 per year working at Belmont Racing Track was not enough for my father to support my mother and my five siblings," Cruz said. "So, my father became an entrepreneur on the side." Cruz's father bought clothing at wholesale prices in Manhattan, then sold it at marked up prices out of his trunk during off hours at the racetrack to make end meets.

They were a closely-knit family. But by eighth grade, young Cruz yearned for a sense of independence. She found it by enrolling at Thomas A. Edison, a different school than her siblings.

Upon graduating from Edison, Cruz was admitted to a highly selective Success Via Apprenticeship (SVA) program that had been launched by New York City Public Schools.[180] The

---

180 "Have A Passion For A Trade? Become A CTE Teacher."

program provided a five-year work and study pathway that qualified Cruz to be a Career and Technical Education (CTE) high school teacher.

Cruz would then spend the next twenty-five years as an award-winning technical education teacher, first at nearby Bushwick High School in Brooklyn, and then at her beloved alma mater, Thomas A. Edison. "I loved my work as a technical educator," Cruz said, "but after a quarter century, I wanted to find a way to have a bigger impact on the trajectory of my students regardless of the career paths they choose."

When the school's principal, Mr. Ojeda, raised the idea of teaching entrepreneurship, Cruz thought back to how much she admired her father for having the creativity and adaptability to support her family as an entrepreneur. Mr. Ojeda explained that teaching in a project-based environment would require a shift in her teaching approach, but Cruz was ready for the challenge.

Immediately, Cruz could see that the classroom dynamics in teaching entrepreneurship were very different because she was putting the students in charge of creating their own business plans. She learned very quickly that she needed to let go of her "sage on the stage" model of transmitting information for her students to memorize. In short order, she began to really enjoy the process of being a "guide on the side," coaching her students through the business planning process.

Cruz's first few years of teaching entrepreneurship went so well that she was asked by Dr. Gold and Rodriguez to be a pilot classroom for the new EMI tool. I asked Cruz to provide an example of how the EMI works in her classroom environment.

Cruz proceeded to tell me a fascinating story of a high school junior named Sheyla Perez. When the EMI was administered to Perez, communication and collaboration stood out as one of the three domains for Perez to improve upon.

In speaking with Perez, Cruz uncovered that her confidence was low in speaking with others because she was not a native English speaker and she was embarrassed about her accent and grammatical errors. Although Perez was very accomplished technically, she was afraid to ask questions in class because of this insecurity. This was stunting her development.

Together, Perez and Cruz created an action plan to improve her communication and collaboration skills over the year-long course during Perez's junior year at Thomas A. Edison. One element of this plan was that Cruz paired Perez up with another student named Carlin for a collaborative exercise on interviewing for a job. Carlin's EMI results indicated that communication and collaboration were a strength, so Cruz asked Carlin to share his expertise with Perez.

It just so happened that Perez was slated to interview for the prestigious New York on Tech[181] internship during her junior year. Her technical competence was outstanding, but she was terrified about the interview. Over the course of several weeks, Carlin played the role of mock interviewer for Perez in the classroom.

Gradually, Perez became more confident and comfortable based upon these and other portions of the program. As a

---

181 "New York on Tech Rebrands to America on Tech to Reflect Its National Expansion."

result, she ended up nailing the interview, got the internship, and is now a thriving computer science major at Queens College. And of course, her post-class EMI test results showed significant improvement.

Here is an excerpt from a letter Perez wrote to Cruz thanking her for developing her Entrepreneurial Mindset in the classroom:

> *Thank you for giving me confidence when I speak out loud. Prior to your class, I always apologized when speaking out loud because I felt like nobody understood me. You showed me that I shouldn't be afraid anymore.*

This is what it looks like when educators like Sandra Cruz apply the EMI in the classroom as part of the project-based entrepreneurship educational experience.

CHAPTER 7

BUILDING THE MINDSET

—

Is it possible to master subject matter in which you have no interest?

This question is at the heart of one of the core principles underlying the project-based entrepreneurship pedagogy. Students get to choose business ideas or social movements based on their individualized interests, not because someone else dictated what they should learn. When students have the freedom to select the projects they embark upon, there is strong evidence to suggest that a more meaningful learning experience occurs.[182]

As a neuroscientist at the Brain and Creativity Institute at the University of Southern California, Dr. Mary Helen Immordino-Yang studied how students' personal connections to topics impact their brain activity. The outcome of her investigation was striking. Dr. Immordino-Yang's analysis demonstrated that when students have an emotional link to what they are learning, heightened activity occurs all around the cortex of their brains, especially in regions involving cognition, memory, and meaning-making.[183]

Her experience as a seventh grade science teacher in Boston prior to becoming a neuroscientist is what drove Dr. Immordino-Yang to pursue this work at the Brain and Creativity Institute. While working as an educator, she became frustrated with the level of engagement from her students.

She began to hypothesize that her students' brain activity must be limited by their lack of emotional ties to the topic.

---

182 Jessica Lahey, "To Help Students Learn, Engage The Emotions."

183 Ibid.

The data from her study consistently validated her theory. "It is literally neurobiologically impossible to think deeply about things that you don't care about," Dr. Immordino-Yang concluded based upon her research.[184]

It turns out that Dr. Immordino-Yang was not the only one discovering this insight and searching for ways to apply it to early education. Some were even seeking to construct pedagogies that tap into the power of passion-driven learning to help students build the sort of mindset they need for the Future of Work.

Given the overwhelming evidence that the Entrepreneurial Mindset is essential for success in the twenty-first century, it is not surprising that a curriculum arose with the explicit design point of enabling young learners to establish this mindset.

ORIGINS OF THE ENTREPRENEURSHIP PATHWAY[185]

It was a cold and snowy February afternoon in 2013 at her office in lower Manhattan. Kimberly Smith had just been hired as NFTE's first Chief Innovation Officer. She was excited to meet with the organization's leadership team to discuss her ideas and priorities in order to align with her team's objectives for the year.

Smith felt confident going into the conversation and eager to share her vision for the future of the institution's program model. A single moment was about to set in motion

---

184 Ibid.

185 "How we do it."

a transformation that would impact the lives of thousands of students.

Moving from Ohio to Colorado during her childhood, Smith often felt like an outsider as an African-American female going to a high school where ninety-eight percent of the population was white. "I became very shy after my parents moved us from multiracial Shaker Heights, Ohio to Engle-wood, Colorado," Smith recounted, "because it was initially challenging for a person of color to connect in a predomi-nantly white community."

In her freshman year of high school, Smith joined Junior Achievement, a nonprofit organization dedicated to prepar-ing young learners for the future by teaching business and networking skills using a student-operated business model. She had always been a creative person—whether it was devel-oping recipes for homemade candy or performing in a play with her neighborhood friends.

At Junior Achievement, her innovative spirit felt welcomed and accepted. She began to form close relationships with her peers over a shared passion for conceiving of business ideas and putting them into action by crafting and executing business plans, selling products, and generating revenue for "shareholders."

This entrepreneurship learning experience was very different for Smith compared to typical classroom environments where it was hard for her to correlate what she learned with how it applied to the "real world." By embracing project-based entrepreneurship education through business creation, Smith felt a sense of personal empowerment that she had not previously known.

Through the process of creating and marketing products ranging from custom candles to auto road repair kits, Smith's shyness gradually faded away and she began to flourish. By her senior year, she had served as an officer in several Junior Achievement companies and ended her senior year as President of her Junior Achievement company.

"Entrepreneurship education in high school was a game-changer for me," Smith said. "When I look back on my experience with Junior Achievement, it is clear that the experience activated a mindset shift that was at the core of who I was but simply needed to be awakened." She had transitioned from a timid teenage girl to a confident young woman who felt optimistic about her ability to innovate, be a leader, and to learn the skills she would need to transition into a career.

Smith would go on to receive a B.S. in Journalism from the University of Colorado and an M.B.A. from Johns Hopkins University. She would also have education leadership roles at the Corporation for Public Broadcasting, Discovery Communications, and the Public Broadcasting Service before landing her role as Chief Innovation Officer at NFTE.

When Smith interviewed with Amy Rosen, NFTE's CEO at the time, Rosen slid the institution's textbook across the table and explained that the book dated back to the 1980s before the rise of the internet. The curriculum was in dire need of a transformation. She asked Smith, "Can you modernize this program?" Smith responded affirmatively to the challenge.

Rosen invited Smith to lead the nonprofit's effort to redesign its curriculum with the aim of activating and developing the Entrepreneurial Mindset in young learners as preparation for the Future of Work. Smith wholeheartedly agreed with Rosen that textbooks alone were no longer adequate to impact a generation of digitally native twenty-first century students.

A journey was thus set in motion to design and implement a comprehensive project-based entrepreneurship education experience that would later become known as the Entrepreneurship Pathway.[186]

CURRICULUM PRINCIPLES

Smith and the team agreed to five organizing principles for the Entrepreneurship Pathway. First, the team decided that the eight domains of the Entrepreneurial Mindset would be emphasized throughout the course work with a weekly cycle of modeling, practicing, and reflecting upon one or more of the mindset components at a time.

"I knew from my own personal experience in high school that the most important aim of the program should be to activate and build the Entrepreneurial Mindset with our students," Smith declared. This theme of focusing on imparting the mindset as the primary aim of the curriculum ultimately carried over into the organization's overall mission which still stands today.

---

186 Ibid.

Second, they would embed a Project-based Learning (PBL)[187] methodology throughout the curriculum whereby students would build a single business concept or social movement throughout their course experience, based on their individual interests.

PBL requires educators to coach more and instruct less, to embrace interdisciplinary learning over focusing on a single subject, and to be more comfortable with ambiguity and discovery during the teaching and learning process. For some teachers, this is a disconcerting departure from the traditional education training they experienced. Change takes time and always comes with challenges.

However, when Smith and her team considered the types of pedagogies that are valuable in preparing students for the Future of Work in the twenty-first century, it was very clear that this learning method was the best option. Based on extensive research, the team selected the Gold Standard PBL model created by the Buck Institute for Education as their approach to building the curriculum.[188]

Third, utilizing research from focus groups with teachers and principals, classroom visits, and an "asset inventory" of the available content, the team determined that a phased pathway of entrepreneurship education was necessary. "We concluded that building a set of progressive course learning experiences where students could advance from one stage to

---

187 "What is PBL?"

188 "Gold Standard PBL."

the next must be a key tenet for the revamped curriculum," Smith said.

The team then began to define a progression, or a sequence, that captured the content standards and competencies, with well-defined beginner, intermediate, and advanced learning experiences. This ultimately became the framework for the multi-year pedagogical approach that defined the Entrepreneurship Pathway. This phased arrangement also addressed the increasing demand from middle schools and high schools looking to implement youth entrepreneurship education across multiple years.

Fourth, Smith and her team determined that the redesign would benefit from a blended learning method that would combine face to face classroom time led by teachers with digital content and tools to support remote learning by students working independently and in groups. The nature of entrepreneurship education requires that students engage in a level of self-driven work to demonstrate their entrepreneurial skills—and the blended learning model supported building student efficacy.

It was important to make the blended learning decision early in the design process. In this way, the team could optimize each instructional element for both classroom collaboration and virtual learning.

Digitizing the curriculum would be a costly and time-consuming process, but it was essential for the nonprofit to meet its pedagogical objectives. And today, with COVID-19 forcing educational institutions everywhere to ramp up their blended learning capacities, these design and investment decisions will benefit students and teachers even more looking forward.

Lastly, it was agreed that students would emerge from the pathway with a credential that recognized their acquired skills, content knowledge, and business competencies. The team researched and identified a set of skill-based assessments and certifications and decided to adopt the Pearson Education Entrepreneurship and Small Business (ESB) certification.[189] The ESB credential is an industry-standard certification developed to test and validate foundation-level concepts and knowledge in entrepreneurship and small business management.

The topics covered on the exam include entrepreneurship; recognizing and evaluating opportunities; planning for, starting, and operating a business; marketing and sales; and financial management. By empowering students to attain this certification by their senior year of high school, this widely recognized credential can then be used in gaining work experience and in applications for post-secondary education.

Today, NFTE's mission is not necessarily to produce students that start their own business as a career path, although that can be a great option for some. Instead, the vision is to activate and instill the mindset of an entrepreneur in young learners in order to equip them for the twenty-first century, irrespective of career path.

The end result of this vigorous and comprehensive effort to redefine the learning value proposition for youth

---

189 "Entrepreneurship and Small Business."

entrepreneurship education was the completion of the highly acclaimed Entrepreneurship Pathway, which now serves as the foundation of the institution's project-based entrepreneurship educational experience.

This year, the Entrepreneurship Pathway will reach tens of thousands of students in the U.S. and around the world.

ORIGINS OF THE ENTREPRENEURSHIP PATHWAY PART II

As Jason Delgatto sat on a park bench outside of Lincoln Park High School on Chicago's north side, he could hardly believe that his dream of becoming a physics teacher was just minutes away from coming true. He had graduated from Northern Illinois University that spring with a degree in physics education.

Delgatto walked into Classroom 104 on that Monday morning in late August of 2004 and waited for the bell to ring. Throughout his K-12 classroom experience as a student growing up in Chicago public schools, Jason had effectively zero exposure to what career paths might be available to him in the future. Like most students, he didn't give much thought to this topic other than an occasional discussion with his parents.

This changed during his junior year of high school when he took physics from an educator that had a unique approach to teaching. Delgatto's teacher used PBL methods whereby each lesson plan was drawn from real-world scenarios so students could see how the curriculum applied outside of the classroom.

For the first time, Delgatto felt inspired in school. As a result, he decided to pursue a college degree that would enable him to become a high school physics educator himself.

As a first-year teacher, Delgatto was handed the task of teaching physics to the lowest academic tier of students at Lincoln Park High School in Chicago. Most of these students came from under-resourced areas near the school.

The graduation rate for this group was about twenty-five percent lower than students in the standard and honors tracks. The administration attributed this sub-standard performance, in part, to lower levels of support and encouragement from the students' parents at home.

These kids also often had less time to study because many worked jobs outside of school to supplement their families' incomes. The assistant principal explained to Delgatto that their only aspiration for these under-performing students was to "get them through the process and hope they find a way to graduate." Despite the challenging circumstances, Delgatto was determined to make a difference.

In his first year, Delgatto followed the school curriculum exactly as it was prescribed. Unfortunately, by the end of the year, he was so frustrated with the lack of responsiveness from his students that he was nearly ready to give up.

"It was a tough introduction to the teaching profession," Delgatto said. "I had big dreams for my students to have the kind of life-altering experience I had with physics in high school, but it became clear that the teaching methods I was using were ineffective." Students simply tuned him out as soon as he began his lectures.

In his second year, Delgatto decided to modify his approach to incorporate the PBL methodology used by his high school teacher that he so admired. He began his first class by asking his students what they were interested in.

Sports and musical entertainment emerged as two common themes, so he set out to teach lessons that demonstrated how physics underpinned each of these arenas. Immediately, students began to respond. It became clear that by identifying projects that were relevant to what his students cared about, he was able to unlock a genuine curiosity they had for learning.

Over the next few years, however, Delgatto started to see that teaching physics, even using PBL tied to students' interests, had limitations. Students were learning more, and test scores were improving, but he was not having the same kind of impact that his high school teacher had.

Delgatto's experience at Lincoln Park High School taught him that a single disciplinary subject like physics was not well-suited for having the broader impact on students' futures that he craved. As a result, he put teaching high school on hold in order to pursue a masters in curriculum studies at DePaul University in search of something more fulfilling.

While at DePaul, Delgatto sought a part-time job that would help pay for school while also keeping him connected to teaching. He found a position as a tutor at a Kaplan center near campus.

Since it was a brand-new center trying to establish itself in the community, Delgatto took the initiative to ask the office director if there was anything he could do to help beyond tutoring. The office director was impressed with Delgatto's ability to recognize the opportunity for growth.

He asked Delgatto if he'd be interested in helping to manage the office as if it was his own business. Delgatto had no previous exposure to entrepreneurship, but he always enjoyed learning new things, so he accepted the challenge.

Delgatto soon found himself digging into the marketing plan to attract new clients and analyzing the profit and loss statement for the office. On one hand, he was frustrated because he felt like he was trying to learn a new language from scratch.

On the other hand, he felt a new sense of freedom and empowerment as he followed his instincts to think creatively about how to grow the business. As time went on, Delgatto began to formulate an idea that perhaps he could combine his curriculum design studies at DePaul with his burgeoning interest in entrepreneurship in a way that could impact the trajectories of young learners' lives in a profound way.

Just as these concepts were coming together in his mind, Delgatto noticed a posting on the DePaul job board from NFTE, an organization that he had not heard of previously. The nonprofit was looking for someone that had teaching experience, expertise in curriculum design, and a passion for entrepreneurship.

"When I saw that job posting," Delgatto recounted, "I knew it was for me." He ultimately got a job offer and later connected with Kim Smith where he served as lead curriculum designer for the Entrepreneurship Pathway under her leadership.

Today, ten years later, Delgatto is still with NFTE where he is more passionate than ever about the power of the project-based entrepreneurship education pedagogy to transform young lives.

A REALITY CHECK

Before we proceed, consider what life would be like if you were an average young person, set to turn eighteen years old this decade.

A lot will change when you reach this age. For the first time, you will be legally considered an adult in nearly every state. You will be able to vote, buy a house, or even get married without restriction in most states.[190] Under other circumstances, you will be able to get sued, gamble away your tuition through online poker, or lose money in the stock market.[191]

High school will come to an end for you. Decisions will need to be made about post-secondary education. You will hear alarming stories about the rising cost of college and about debt loads taken on by students now struggling to make loan payments.[192] You will learn that, under current policy,

---

190 Jackie Burrell, "Laws to Remember When You Legally Become an Adult at 18."

191 Ibid.

192 Harmeet Kaur, "The student loan debt is $1.6 trillion, and people are struggling to pay it down."

student debt can't be eliminated even if you are forced to file for bankruptcy, except in extreme cases.[193]

You may decide that community college is a more cost-effective option. And with social distancing policies resulting from COVID-19, you may be more likely to consider credentials obtained through virtual learning as a compliment to or even replacement of the traditional college experience.

Your parents will no longer be legally obligated to provide for you financially when you turn eighteen, so earning money and determining a career path will begin to take center stage in your life. But, the world of work will look drastically different than the one in which your parents began their careers.

Intelligent machines will take over many of the jobs that used to be done by people in your age range.[194] You will need to understand how to think and act like an entrepreneur in the Gig Economy. Having a "side hustle" as an entrepreneur will probably be the best way for you to earn extra money to help pay for school and living expenses.[195] Remote work will be more commonplace as a consequence of COVID-19, requiring that you find creative ways to develop relationships and build your personal network.[196]

---

193 "Myth Busted: Turns Out Bankruptcy Can Wipe Out Student Loan Debt After All."

194 Manyika and Chui, "Harnessing automation for a future that works."

195 James Wellemeyer, "One-third of Americans say they need a side gig to pay expenses."

196 Deborah Mackenzie, "Our chance to contain the coronavirus may already be over."

You will almost certainly be genuinely concerned about the environment. You will be keenly aware of sweeping societal challenges through your vast access to information on the internet and social media. You will likely be cynical about the behavior of older generations that led to environmental pollution and extreme wealth inequality.[197]

You will probably find yourself searching for ways to maintain a sense of optimism in politically divisive surroundings.[198] You very well may lean toward supporting a socialist agenda over capitalism if you do not see businesses acting with a higher level of conscientiousness.[199]

What kinds of educational experiences would you want to have completed by the time you finish high school, knowing that this is what it will be like to become an adult in the 2020s? Are the current teaching methods and curricula offered by our middle and high schools enough to equip you to enter adulthood in the twenty-first century?

MIDDLE SCHOOL CURRICULUM DESIGN

The questions from this "reality check" weigh heavily on Delgatto's mind today as he leads design for NFTE's Entrepreneurship Pathway. I asked Delgatto to provide a synopsis of the curriculum, and to outline how he would implement youth entrepreneurship education if it were entirely up to

---

197 Nicole Lyn Pesce, "Chart shows jaw-dropping wealth gap between millennials and boomers."

198 Colton Carpenter, "The Divided United States of America."

199 Morgan Gstalter, "7 in 10 millennials say they would vote for a socialist."

him. Delgatto started the discussion with middle schools (ages eleven to thirteen).

"One thing we consistently see is that digitally native middle school students are far more capable than ever before of turning their creative ideas into viable business concepts," Delgatto revealed. He explained that the ubiquity of information and the familiarity with easy-to-use digital tools has significantly altered how much students at this age can achieve within learning environments that elicit their creative energy.

In fact, he has seen examples of students below the age of ten achieve extraordinary results through project-based entrepreneurship education. But, for now, the organization is primarily focused at the middle and high school levels, while recognizing that the pedagogy can be adapted to serve learners before middle school and beyond high school as well.

The challenge for middle schools, Delgatto said, is that often they don't have as much flexibility in their schedules as high schools do. Teaching basic academics, often coupled with an enhanced focus on STEM, leaves little room for additional topics.

For this reason, NFTE has focused mainly on awareness of and exposure to pedagogical elements that provide snippets of project-based entrepreneurship education at the middle school level. For example, the nonprofit hosts virtual events throughout the school year called the World Series of Innovation, typically alongside a sponsoring corporate partner.

Students are asked to form teams of two to three people that together create and submit a sixty-second video on their plan to solve a social problem. Challenges generally stem from the Sustainable Development Goals (SDGs) developed in 2015 by the United Nations, such as climate action, good health & well-being, and gender equality.[200] In this way, middle school students get some initial familiarity with collaborative PBL, problem solving, and creative thinking through the lens of Conscious Capitalism.

Delgatto recalls one World Series of Innovation that focused on finding solutions to forest fires impacting California. Teams of students came back with video presentations conceptualizing the use of software to predict high risk areas, sensors to detect early signs of fires, and drones to pour water on fires and perform search and rescue missions.

"It is extraordinary to see how well middle school students can identify opportunities to apply technology when these sorts of PBL scenarios are made available to them," Delgatto said. "Most don't yet have the technical skills to develop the solutions, but they are very capable of conceptualizing innovative approaches to solve problems."

NFTE provides a toolkit for students to utilize for the World Series of Innovation and a framework that includes two ninety-minute guided sessions that cover the idea to execution process. The student-crafted videos are then scored by a virtual panel of judges from the sponsoring organization, and feedback is provided to each team.

---

200 "Sustainable Development Goals."

The three finalists then go head-to-head in a public, online vote. The public's votes are combined with the judges' scores to select one winning team. Prize money from the sponsor is awarded based on the order in which teams finish.

Another example of a program for middle schools is called Venture. In collaboration with a partner, NFTE created an interactive experience that shows students how to start a virtual food truck business. Students are guided through the business planning process step by step.

At the end, students that took the initiative to complete the entire process receive their own e-Portfolio which includes a dynamic, visual representation of the business plan they created. The students also discuss which aspects of the Entrepreneurial Mindset were most applicable in enabling them to craft their business plans as a precursor to further mindset development in high school.

A third example is called Start-Up Tech which is sponsored in part by SAP.[201] In this program, NFTE provides a PBL scenario that has students build a digital solution to improve their local community in an innovative way that showcases the values of Conscious Capitalism.

The MIT App Inventor, which is designed specifically for beginners,[202] is used over the course of a semester to generate the app. A guided online tool is also used by students to build a high-level summary of their business plans.

---

201 Roberto Torres, "This program helps high-schoolers find their way to tech."

202 "With MIT App Inventor, anyone can build apps with global impact."

A lean business plan canvas and the final app are then presented virtually through an online expo where winners receive prize money and publicity. In this way, students and teachers get exposure to PBL that is blended across the disciplines of entrepreneurship and software coding. Open discussions are also encouraged about which dimensions of the Entrepreneurial Mindset were most critical in facilitating the creation of the app and business plan.

These and other middle school programs serve as a catalyst to begin building the Entrepreneurial Mindset in students in the eleven- to thirteen-year-old age range, while inspiring them to pursue more advanced stages of youth entrepreneurship education in high school.

HIGH SCHOOL CURRICULUM DESIGN

For high school students (ages fourteen to eighteen), the Entrepreneurship Pathway curriculum has two year-long courses called Entrepreneurship 1 & 2 which are ideally suited for students during their sophomore and junior years. I asked Delgatto to elaborate on the design and implementation of the curriculum at the high school level.

The first recommendation he made is for high school boards to consider an introduction to career pathways course during students' freshman year. "A major factor that determines the success of the project-based entrepreneurship curriculum is the ability for students to choose a strong business idea for which they have an innate passion," he said. Delgatto explained that exposing students to industries and the dynamics of the Future of Work, with an emphasis on new and emerging career categories, is a best practice for completion prior to Entrepreneurship 1.

Delgatto cited the LifePath Career Exploration Course as an example of what he suggests for students during their freshman year. This seventeen-module course provides a standalone, comprehensive career guidance resource that can be implemented as student led, independent study or through teacher-directed, classroom use.[203]

During the course, students examine their strengths and weaknesses and use this as context for exploring and researching career opportunities, including a focus on sixteen basic career clusters and related industry credentials. They learn the basics of building mentor relationships, communications, and ethics in a workplace environment along with skills such as résumé design, cover letter writing, job prospecting, and interviewing. The course concludes with a module on financial literacy to highlight the importance of this subject, regardless of whatever career pathways are ultimately chosen by students.

This type of coursework provides an important foundation to get students thinking about areas of interest. It also gets them comfortable with the notion of setting goals around career pathways and the pursuit of post-secondary education in a manner that aligns with students' strengths and passions, while also factoring in key market dynamics.

---

203 "LifePath Career Exploration Course."

Entrepreneurship 1

Entrepreneurship 1 is designed as a full-year project-based entrepreneurship educational experience, ideally suited for a student's sophomore year in high school. It can also be implemented as a summer school program, after school program, or it can be embedded piecemeal into schools' preexisting curricula using a modular approach.

The classroom experience takes a student through an entrepreneurial journey, pursuing a business opportunity of their own creation. Students use lean startup principles to build, validate, and present their individual ideas to panels of judges as part of a local, regional, and nationally organized entrepreneurship competition called the Youth Entrepreneurship Challenge.

"The course begins with an overview of the eight domains of the Entrepreneurial Mindset, followed by the completion of the EMI diagnostic tool to assess strengths and weaknesses within each domain," Delgatto observed. Each week, one of the eight components is emphasized, and personalized learning is used throughout the project to underscore strengths and boost areas of improvement across the domains.

Here is a high-level synopsis of the major curriculum components within Entrepreneurship 1:

1. Operation Mindset

Students get an engaging look at what it means to think and act like an entrepreneur in a series of four challenges—each designed to activate two of the eight aspects of the Entrepreneurial Mindset. At the end of the module, students learn about the characteristics of an entrepreneur before doing their own self-assessment of their propensity for entrepreneurial thinking using the EMI.

2. Developing the Entrepreneurial Mindset
Students learn what it means to solve problems like an entrepreneur. They gain insight into how entrepreneurs provide business solutions to problems held by individuals and businesses, as well as social problems facing local, national, and global communities.

3. Testing an Opportunity
Students learn about the difference between an idea and a true business opportunity. Instruction takes students through the process of validating their business solution through market research with an emphasis on lean startup methodologies, testing assumptions, and iterative design principles.

4. Building a Competitive Edge
Students learn about basic economic concepts and the role these play in the success of a business. Students also assemble competitor profiles and a competitive matrix to determine advantage within their industry.

5. Creating Your Biggest Fans
Students look at the importance of assembling a marketing plan and approaches for crafting customer profiles for their target customer segments. With a focus on modern and cost-effective strategies, students put together their planned go-to-market channels to customers and the key metrics they will use to measure the effectiveness of these channels.

6. Making a Profit

Students learn about the various expenses incurred by a business and how entrepreneurs do an analysis of unit economics to help predict the overall profitability of the business. This segment teaches students how to calculate markup in a distribution channel, their profit per unit after their variable expenses, and a break-even analysis against their ongoing fixed expenses.

7. Pitch Competition

Students use their lean canvas and business plan artifacts to put together an opportunity pitch deck. Students prepare and present their potential business opportunities to judges in organized local, regional, and national competitions.

8. Pivot or Persevere

Students debrief on the competition, and they can adjust their lean canvas based upon judges' feedback. Students also think about their own post-secondary pathway to success, and how their business opportunity could be utilized toward applying to college and for career aspirations.

In completing Entrepreneurship 1, and through participating in the organized entrepreneurship competition, students work to advance the eight domains of the Entrepreneurial Mindset every step of the way. Furthermore, by going through the process of developing a plan for their own companies, students gain valuable experiential learning that facilitates a deeper understanding about how companies in existence today originated in essentially the same way.

Entrepreneurship 2

Entrepreneurship 2 is also a full-year entrepreneurship educational experience, particularly well-suited for a high school student's junior year. In this course, students form teams around the most feasible business opportunities gleaned from Entrepreneurship 1.

These groups then work collaboratively to build prototypes and create comprehensive operational, financing, and go-to-market business plans. At the end of the course, the projects are presented by each team to investor panels that are empowered to provide seed money grants to the most deserving businesses.

"Students that complete Entrepreneurship 2 are also fully equipped to pass the Entrepreneurship and Small Business (ESB) certification," Delgatto said. The ESB is a widely recognized industry credential that is valuable in applying to college, pursuing work experience, and in demonstrating students' commitment to advancing each domain of the Entrepreneurial Mindset.[204]

Here is a high-level overview of the major curriculum elements in Entrepreneurship 2:

1. Growing the Entrepreneurial Mindset: Leadership & Teamwork

Students participate in a series of challenges that require them to work as a team to solve complex problems. Students reflect on the entrepreneurial skills they used in the experiential activities as well as their opportunities for growth.

---

204 "Entrepreneurship and Small Business."

2. Achieving a Product-Market Fit

Students work collaboratively to develop a minimum viable product (MVP). As part of this effort, they get out of the classroom and conduct A/B testing with potential customers to validate product-market fit. A/B testing is a way to compare two versions of a single variable, typically by testing a subject's response to variant A against variant B, and then determining which of the two variants is more effective. Students also work on product development and market positioning during this curriculum element.

3. Designing a Business Model

Students conduct online research and learn about distribution channels, internal resourcing, and external ecosystem partnerships that can accelerate profitable growth for the business. Students also learn about and consider how to structure their business in order to optimize performance of key metrics.

4. Utilizing Digital Marketing and Sales

Students learn about online and offline selling and marketing strategies. They develop a website and a social media campaign to market their business and, if appropriate, begin to sell their products.

5. Planning for Business Operations

Students learn about human capital, intellectual property, basic record keeping, and basic accounting. Students also consider the importance of ethics and how they can create socially responsible, sustainable businesses that are consistent with the principles of Conscious Capitalism.

6. Financing a Startup

Students develop financial ratios and a projected income statement for their business. They learn about boot strapping, crowd sourcing, equity capital, and using loans to finance their business. Students also learn about the importance of maintaining credit scores.

7. Managing a Small Business

Students learn about human resources, government regulations, and taxes relevant to their business and how to comply with these laws as part of the preparation necessary for the ESB certification exam.

Winning teams proceed to launch their business with seed capital grants. Students can also opt to earn the ESB certification. Delgatto urges students to invest the additional time to attain the ESB credential to further establish their pledge to advancing each element of the Entrepreneurial Mindset in preparation for the twenty-first century economy.

He also reiterated that the project-based entrepreneurship education pedagogy is actively being tested for age ranges beyond the current scope with very encouraging results. While Entrepreneurship 1 & 2 are ideal for high school students to complete before graduation, he was careful to allow for alternative scenarios where the curriculum can be applied to additional age ranges. One promising new potential segment, for example, is community colleges. And with the impact of COVID-19, creative virtual learning experiences are also likely to be utilized more broadly.

CONCLUSION

The Entrepreneurship Pathway curriculum is designed to help young learners build the Entrepreneurial Mindset starting in middle school and extending through high school (and perhaps through community colleges or other avenues in the future). Both full-year courses (E1 & E2) begin with exploration and measurement of the eight elements of the mindset. Each week, one mindset domain is emphasized to drive improvement throughout the educational experience.

The curriculum is highly adaptable, so that it can be taught stand-alone or through integration into pre-existing courses. Students that complete Entrepreneurship 1 & 2 are fully prepared to earn the ESB certification. This is a very useful credential for gaining work experience, applying to college, and signaling commitment to continuously develop the Entrepreneurial Mindset.

CHAPTER 8

CONNECTING TO THE REAL WORLD

—

$1.7 trillion dollars.[205]

This is the amount of student loan debt from higher education that is suffocating 45 million Americans.[206] Some may carry these loan payments throughout the majority of their lives.[207] Even if the federal government steps in to address this debt issue, the education to career system in the U.S. is still very broken.[208]

One of the root causes of this devastating problem is that students often don't know why they are going to college in the first place.[209] Most get little exposure to the "real world" in middle and high school in ways that bring to light career options and pathways. And would-be volunteer mentors often find it difficult to identify a starting point to help young students in a manner that meets them where they are.[210]

A unique attribute of the entrepreneurship education pedagogy is that the business planning project provides a natural way for students to connect with mentors. Beyond receiving coaching on their business plans, students often learn about career fields related to their chosen topics through these external relationships.

---

205 "Student Loan Debt Clock."

206 Zach Friedman, "Student Loan Debt Statistics In 2020: A Record $1.6 Trillion."

207 Michelle Singletary, "There seems to be no end to the rise in student load debt."

208 "Our Education System Is Broken…And 3 Ways To Fix It."

209 Horn and Moesta, *Choosing College: How To Make Better Learning Decisions Throughout Your Life.*

210 "Challenges and Lessons Learned."

As a result, more informed decisions can be made to identify the most suitable post-secondary education options and work experience. Empowered with a clearer view of how their post-secondary education will advance their career interests, young learners are better positioned to maximize the return on their investments in education and thrive in the workforce.

Let's explore some examples of how project-based entrepreneurship education enables young people to connect with the "real world" in distinctly beneficial ways. Establishing these relationships early and often is a vital aspect of developing the Entrepreneurial Mindset and helping young learners prepare for the Future of Work.

MENTOR CONNECTIONS

It was Thanksgiving week of 1998 in her home state of Maryland, but NFTE board member and Lifetime Volunteer Achievement award winner Patty Alper[211] was struggling to feel thankful. It had been a difficult year of coping with tragedy in her family. Alper had always been deeply spiritual, but this Thanksgiving seemed void of meaning. After a twenty-minute radio interview with a fourteen-year-old from an under-resourced community in nearby Washington D.C., Alper's spirits were lifted, and the direction of her life would soon be altered forever.

Following her graduation from Cornell College in Mount Vernon, Iowa with a degree in English and Theology, Alper

---

211 "Patty Alper Honored With NFTE Lifetime Volunteer Achievement Award."

worked for the state's Juvenile Detention Center system. There, she counseled incarcerated youth with the goal of readying them to return to society as productive citizens.

Like most states in the U.S., Iowa had difficulty with recidivism whereby prisoners return to jail for repeatedly committing crime. "I felt a strong sense of fulfillment in helping these young prisoners truly connect with an adult that, honestly, didn't look anything like them," Alper said.

Returning to her home state a few years later, Alper then worked at a psychiatric hospital called Chestnut Lodge to counsel mentally ill adolescents. Here too she had a meaningful impact on the lives of others and made a positive contribution to society.

As time went on, however, Alper determined that she was ready for new ventures that were less weighty and problematic. It was time for a career change.

She found her calling as an entrepreneur. Together with her business partners, she founded a project management company specializing in building corporate headquarter facilities and high-end interiors for large businesses in the Washington, D.C. metro area. Over the next decade, she grew the business to over $50 million in annual revenue as the partner in charge of development. As one of the first woman-owned founders in the industry, Alper was widely recognized as a rain maker, winning numerous projects exceeding 200,000 square feet along the way.

But as her business flourished over the years, she felt herself moving further away from the purpose-driven work that had been so rewarding at the outset of her career. Seeking to rediscover this feeling of personal fulfillment, Alper started a theological study group in her own home.

The small group studied thinkers from the modern era all the way back to ancient philosophers from BC. In one particular year, her group studied the teachings of Maimonides, a twelfth-century Jewish philosopher.

Through this exploration, Alper became captivated with a concept espoused by Maimonides called the hierarchy of tzedakah.[212] The philosophy profiled eight levels of charitable giving and sequenced them according to their significance.

She was familiar with Maslow's hierarchy of needs, but she had never seen a framework like this applied to giving back to others. At the top of Maimonides' hierarchy is the important concept to empower those in need to be able to live without financial or survival support from others.

Raised in the Jewish tradition, Alper believed this revelation did not occur by accident, especially since a family foundation had recently been formed through which she could give. "In that moment, I felt a renewed sense of spiritual direction. As I searched for new ways of giving back, I knew that I must find a means to reach the top of Maimonides' pyramid," she said. But the question remained as to how Alper could have the biggest impact.

And then came that fateful Thanksgiving week of 1998. As a result of her success in business, Alper had been able to

---

212 "Maimonedes' Eight Level of Charity."

start a radio show that she hosted and produced herself. That Thanksgiving week, she had invited several NFTE students and staff to come on air.

One of her guests on the program that week was a fourteen-year-old girl named Janelle Stubbs who had created a business plan for a stained-glass window company. In the twenty-minute on-air conversation that ensued, Alper was blown away by Janelle's acumen, trajectory, and life skills. Alper had never considered that a fourteen-year-old could have such a well-formulated business plan and be so astute in answering pointed questions about her strategy.

As part of the show, Alper learned much more about NFTE, it's programs and it's prodigies like Janelle Stubbs. As she began to grasp the incredible influence entrepreneurship education had on this young student's life, Alper had an epiphany.

She could take her own experience as an entrepreneur and use it to mentor young students just like Janelle. She would teach them to become self-sufficient in line with the guidance provided by Maimonides' pyramid. A new mission had been born in Alper's life.

Alper started by visiting students once a month in D.C. area high schools to mentor them on their business plans. She played devil's advocate to their ideas, coached them on how to present their pitches to judges, and encouraged them to launch their ideas into businesses with real profits.

As she built relationships with these students, she could see how hungry they were to have this outside perspective.

Toward the end of each course, teachers would ask their students to write letters of appreciation to their mentors. It was these letters, now 2,500 strong, that inspired Alper to write her book called *Teach to Work: How a Mentor, A Mentee, and a Project Can Close the Skills Gap in America.*

Here is a short excerpt from the book where Alper wrote about the wisdom she gained from working with these young students:

> *I am certain of this: students want to find ways to connect to a world that they suspect is quite different from either school or home. They need to feel connected to a world that looks complex and maybe incoherent. Instead of fear and rejection, boredom and memorization, a mentor's picture can offer an alternative pathway in a student's mind's eye.*[213]

As Alper's volunteer efforts grew, it became clear that just about every student in every class she visited wanted the kind of counsel she was providing. It was equally clear that there were so many people in her generation that wanted to give back by sharing their business experience with young people.

In order to connect young students with mentors, Alper came up with the idea to create an Adopt-a-Class program. The program would have business leaders like herself take on a lead mentor role for an entire high school entrepreneurship class throughout the school year.

---

213 Patty Alper, *Teach to Work: How a Mentor, a Mentee, and a Project Can Close the Skills Gap in America*, chap. 3.

Fast forward to today, and Alper has personally reached nearly 2,000 students in the D.C. area through her program. Based on the model Alper developed, the program grew to be in twelve cities across the U.S. at its height.

The power of mentoring young people through project-based entrepreneurship education has become crystal clear through these initiatives. Alper summed it up this way in another excerpt from *Teach to Work:*

> *Mentors hold a unique power to transform a student's life. This has been my experience and my passion. I am witness to its impact firsthand with my own mentees for fifteen years (now over 20). But in doing research I've learned that I am not alone—many others view mentoring relationships as central to education and human development. The more I learn, the more I wonder why it is not more universal as part of the American educational experience.*[214]

And herein lies the key point about mentoring students through project-based entrepreneurship education. It should be a standard part of the learning experience for all students, not just a select few. In this way, we can build the Entrepreneurial Mindset in young learners prior to adulthood, and therefore equip them to prosper in the 21st century economy.

---

214 Ibid.

CAREER CONNECTIONS
Your career is just one click away.

This is how easy 2019 NFTE Volunteer of the Year award winners Nick Hare and Heather Wetzler intend to make it for young people to explore career opportunities.[215] As a husband and wife team, they started a company called Cue Career to make this happen at scale. Let's put them to the test.

One of the hottest new fields in which young people can begin their careers is called user experience (UX) design. This industry has seen rapid growth due to the proliferation of mobile devices.

To see how potent Cue Career can be, go to YouTube and type in "UX designer Cue Career." A video will pop up that has been viewed over 100,000 times. The clip is a seven-minute interview between a young student and a member of the User Experience Professional Association (UXPA) named Riana who is also a freelance UX designer and a Georgia Tech graduate.

In the YouTube interview, Riana outlines a "day in the life of" a UX designer. She talks about the skills that are needed to begin a career in UX design and how to acquire them. She explains the importance of attaining industry credentials that are appealing to employers. Riana also shares where to look for gigs and how to connect with the UX Professional Association to learn more.[216]

---

215 "Two Top Businesses in Los Angeles Metro Youth Entrepreneurship Challenge Will Go to Nationals."

216 Cue Career, "Freshman Intern Interviews Riana about UX Design Career."

She then refers the student to the UXPA website. Here, the student can find resources, publications, events, local chapters, and contact information of people that can answer questions about the industry.[217]

I tried this YouTube search as an experiment. It worked beautifully. I also went to the Cue Career website where I found the same sorts of easy to consume videos free of charge across a wide range of industries. The experience was fantastic.

Nick Hare, who serves as CEO of Cue Career, shared his personal story for founding the company. He dropped out of the University of Wisconsin after his freshman year because he didn't want to incur debt for a degree in something that wasn't relevant to his future.

"When I think back to my high school years in Green Bay, Wisconsin," Hare recounted, "it would have been so great to have Cue Career to help me identify interesting careers. It took me five years and seven jobs after dropping out of college to figure this out, and only then did I feel comfortable investing in post-secondary education." In Hare's case, this decision to defer college turned out to be a wise one.

Hare went back to the University of Wisconsin once he understood that he had a passion for helping cities become more sustainable in order to combat climate change. He earned a B.S. in Geography, and then went on to the University of Texas for an M.S. in Urban Planning. These degrees were instrumental in him landing a position with the City of Santa

---

217 "User Experience Professionals Association."

Monica where he spent nearly a decade as superintendent overseeing policies to improve the city's sustainability.

As a result of Hare's leadership, the city has won numerous awards for moving to renewable sources of energy, reducing water consumption, and preventing plastics from being deposited into the ocean. It was a tremendously rewarding decade for Hare.

He would not have been able to get the job without earning the degrees he attained. Empowered with this understanding in advance, Hare pursued post secondary education that provided an exceptional return on his investment.

When Hare and Wetzler began dating in 2014, they formed a bond over the struggles they each had had trying to match their passions with careers that best suited them. Through research and conversations with friends and colleagues, Hare and Wetzler concluded that trade associations were a hidden gem in addressing the challenges they had experienced.

"You hardly ever hear people talk about trade associations as a solution to the massive education to career gap in our country," Wetzler declared. "But in fact, this is a $150 billion industry, and each association is a tremendously valuable resource for anyone looking to break into an industry or job function." And as active participants in their industries, trade associations must continuously stay current with trends which reinforces their value proposition.

The problem was that there was no single, easy to use platform to connect young people to the vast resources that trade associations offer. Cue Career is designed to solve this problem.

One of the lessons Hare and Wetzler have learned in working with NFTE students is that project-based entrepreneurship education at the middle and high school levels is an ideal means through which students can connect with platforms like Cue Career. In this way, young learners quickly gain industry connections to enhance their business planning projects. And once a student watches a Cue Career video, they see how easy it is to explore careers in their areas of interest now and in the future.

Today, Cue Career serves tens of thousands of students, job seekers, and trade associations through its platform. The biggest challenge is awareness that Cue Career exists in the first place. Hare and Wetzler both firmly believe that we must instill the Entrepreneurial Mindset in young learners to help them see that platforms like Cue Career are out there to help them build bridges to their futures.

Those that apply the Entrepreneurial Mindset by utilizing resources like Cue Career early and often will be well equipped to prosper in the Future of Work.

CONNECTING TO REAL-WORLD EXPERIENCE

In the summer of 2012, Angela Miceli had a decision to make.

She had spent two decades working for an engineering firm in Chicago, where she had grown up. Miceli had successfully risen from an intern payroll clerk to controller during her tenure at the company. Leading the implementation of a new financial system for the company following a merger that doubled the size of the organization was her signature achievement.

Miceli was immensely proud of her accomplishments, and she developed many friendships along the way. However, she was in search of a higher purpose for her career rather than continuing down the same path.

Growing up in the Chicago area, Miceli worked exceptionally hard in school. However, it really bothered her that she had spent so much of her childhood memorizing facts in order to recite them on tests.

"Looking back, I really felt trapped inside of a system that rewarded test taking over real-world problem solving and creative thinking," Miceli said. By the time she graduated high school, Miceli was completely burned out and even resentful of school.

Miceli's frustration with her early education led her to the conclusion that a university setting was not right for her. She recalls a moment when one of her classmates who studied far less but performed better on standardized tests got admitted to the college she had once dreamed of attending. This upset her deeply because Miceli worked much harder and got better grades, but the university did not seem to care.

Instead of seeking a four-year college degree, Miceli chose to attend a junior college that prided itself on preparing students for career readiness and placing them in specific jobs. She earned an associate degree in computerized business systems which led directly to her payroll clerk internship at the engineering firm where she then spent two decades.

As she reflected upon her schooling and her career in business, Miceli began to develop a yearning to give back to young people that were experiencing the same kind of disillusionment with school that she had faced. "It became obvious to me that the skills that led to my success in business had very little to do with the facts I had spent so much time memorizing during my early education," Miceli said. Instead, Miceli attributed her achievements in business to her ability to identify opportunities to improve profitability, creative problem solving, and being able to communicate and collaborate within teams of people with diverse backgrounds and skill sets.

Miceli wanted to find a way to teach these skills to young people that also felt trapped in the school system, just as she had growing up. A turning point came when the *Chicago Tribune* ran a story about the "Friends for a Future" program at Holy Trinity High School located near downtown Chicago.

The school's President, Timothy Bopp, was hailed as a visionary for building connections between his high school students and business leaders in Chicago. One by one, Bopp developed personal relationships with executives and convinced them that his high school students would make great interns.

He told them that internships would be a way for their companies to give back to their community, as well providing real-world business experience to the next generation. Ultimately, Bopp formalized this into an internship program which he called "Friends for a Future."[218]

---

218 "Summer Programs."

As the program gained traction and enthusiasm grew as a result of the *Chicago Tribune's* reporting, so did the school's interest in hiring teachers with a strong track record of business experience. Through a common acquaintance, Miceli got connected with Bopp, and from there she could sense that the timing was right for her to transition into teaching. Miceli was hired by Holy Trinity as a math teacher at first, and soon thereafter she was asked to teach a course on corporate experience to share her business expertise with students.

About the same time, an advisory board member of Holy Trinity had heard about NFTE and suggested to Bopp that they consider bringing the program into the school. As Miceli became more familiar with entrepreneurship education, she could see that it encapsulated exactly the kinds of aptitudes that led to her success in business. She believed that these capacities would become even more important given the increasingly rapid pace of technological automation.

Miceli had found her new mission. She would focus on developing the Entrepreneurial Mindset in her students at Holy Trinity using the project-based entrepreneurship education pedagogy. In this way, she could bring her twenty years of experience in business to her students, while also helping them see that there is a much bigger world outside beyond memorizing facts and taking tests.

When Miceli met with Bopp, she suggested that they bring together the "Friends for a Future" internship program with the project-based entrepreneurship curriculum. She could then match students to internship opportunities based upon their areas of interest.

Companies would benefit from digital native students bringing in fresh ideas, while her students could take away lessons learned from their internships and incorporate them into their business plans. Bopp agreed wholeheartedly, and the two programs were merged.

Six years later, Miceli has become one of the most accomplished teachers in the NFTE network. She is now an NFTE Master Educator qualified to train other teachers as they enter the program.[219]

In 2019, two of the three national finalists for the Youth Entrepreneurship Challenge business planning competition came from Miceli's classroom. Considering that tens of thousands of students participate each year, this was a truly extraordinary achievement, and a testament to the impact Miceli is having with her students.

Through the "Friends for a Future" program, Miceli gets great feedback from business leaders in Chicago on how to continuously improve her approach to better prepare her students for the Future of Work in the twenty-first century. These executives tell Miceli that she is right on track with her focus on building the Entrepreneurial Mindset to her students.

Executives in Chicago also stress that in hiring young people, they want to see tangible examples of students taking the initiative to identify real-world problems and creatively solving these problems by working collaboratively in teams.

219 "Recognition and Leadership Opportunities."

They explain that demonstrating this real-world experience is often the difference between who gets hired and who doesn't.

This is music to Miceli's ears because it is exactly what she is doing with her students every day. She believes this model of combining classroom learning with real-world experience, often referred to as apprenticeship or internship programs, can scale widely across the U.S. as it has in Europe.[220]

In leaving the corporate world to focus on sharing her business experience with young people through project-based entrepreneurship education, Angela Miceli has found the new sense of purpose she sought. You can bet that her students will be among the best prepared for the twenty-first century economy.

CONNECTING THROUGH CORPORATE VOLUNTEERISM

Growing up in the small town of Newark, Ohio, 2019 NFTE Volunteer of the Year Award winner Alex Van Atta[221] was raised with volunteerism as a core value in his family. Together with his parents and siblings, Van Atta regularly participated in giving back to their community through the local food pantry, for example. In doing so, his parents explained that caring for the least fortunate among us is our highest calling as human beings.

In high school, Van Atta was a National Honor Society award winner as a result of his extensive volunteer efforts.

---

220 Matt Krupnick, "U.S. Goes To School For Apprenticeships."

221 "Slalom's Alex Van Atta Named Entrepreneurship Volunteer of the Year."

In college at Northwestern University, he became a Fellow at the Center for Civic Engagement where they focused on connecting students to nonprofits in the area. When it was time to enter the workforce after college, however, Van Atta was concerned that his passion for volunteerism would need to be put on hold given the intense demands of his chosen field of technology consulting.

Van Atta's job search went on for months during his senior year, and at times it seemed like it would be impossible to find a company where he could be a meaningful contributor to his community while travelling from client to client for consulting projects. Just as he began to feel hopeless about the prospects of trying to balance volunteerism with consulting, he learned about Slalom, a global consulting firm focused on strategy, technology, and business transformation.[222]

The firm has a unique locally-focused model wherein consultants get staffed only on projects for local clients in order to minimize travel and maintain work-life balance. Van Atta knew this was the company for him and he gratefully accepted a job with Slalom's Chicago office when it was offered.

Upon joining the firm, Van Atta was immediately drawn to NFTE's Adopt-a-Class program which had been embraced by Slalom. "I had not been exposed to project-based entrepreneurship education at the middle or high school level before, but my colleagues raved about the mentor relationships they had built through bringing their experiences to young people as they developed their business plans," Van Atta said.

---

222 "Redefine what's possible."

He decided to give it a try.

After his first session coaching students at a local Chicago high school, Van Atta was hooked. In just a short time, he could sense the creative energy he had inspired in the young people with whom he collaborated.

As Van Atta continued his volunteer efforts and became more convinced of the impact that he was having in serving under-resourced youth through entrepreneurship education, he began to wonder if Slalom could go above and beyond the regular Adopt-a-Class program. There was a high school in a small town in Northwest Indiana that offered entrepreneurship education and caught his attention because it reminded him of where he grew up in Newark, Ohio.

"I knew the feeling of being in an isolated small town growing up, so I wanted to find a way to help these kids feel more connected," Van Atta said. It would be difficult for Slalom consultants in Chicago to travel to schools that far away for a mentor program, but he thought that perhaps he could use technology to offer mentoring virtually.

And that is exactly what Van Atta did.

As part of a Slalom event, REALIZE, that brought together business and community leaders in Chicago, Van Atta created a new program for entrepreneurship students from far-away schools to record and submit their business pitches through videos. He then set up booths at the REALIZE event for business leaders to view the videos and provide their feedback verbally.

Using sophisticated voice-to-text technology, the viewer's comments were automatically converted to text and sent to students. Over fifty students participated in the first year and they were thrilled to get insights from some of the most prominent business leaders in Chicago.[223]

With the pilot phase of the virtual mentoring model complete, Van Atta plans to apply the framework to a broader group of entrepreneurship students in the future. And with increased adoption of virtual learning in response to COVID-19, the approach may become even more applicable than originally envisioned.

Slalom is also looking to leverage the use case in future engagements with its partners and clients. When organizations cultivate a culture of volunteerism and help invest in youth entrepreneurship education, it can inspire innovation that can be applied to the business itself.

Alex Van Atta is a shining example demonstrating how this rings true.

CONCLUSION

The business planning project in the entrepreneurship education pedagogy provides an ideal means for young learners to connect to the "real world" through mentor relationships. The benefits of establishing these connections early and often go far beyond coaching to improve business plans.

---

223 Alex Van Atta, "How Slalom and NFTE Used AI and Machine Learning to Mentor High School Entrepreneurs."

Mentors become sounding boards to align interests expressed by students through their business plans with their pursuits of higher education, internships, and career pathways. These network effects are another key ingredient that makes project-based entrepreneurship education the quintessential learning method for developing the Entrepreneurial Mindset and preparing young people for the Future of Work.

CHAPTER 9

TWENTY-FIRST CENTURY HEROES

———

Who are your heroes?

I had the good fortune of attending NFTE's annual teacher summit in the summer of 2019 in Chicago. I was astounded by the level of enthusiasm emanating from this group of 200 high school educators from around the U.S.

There was not a single teacher I met that was not overflowing with joy about the positive impact they are having on their students. The stories they shared about changing students' mindsets and altering the trajectories of their lives were remarkable.

According to Merriam-Webster, a hero is defined as a person who is admired or idealized for courage, outstanding achievements, or noble qualities.[224] I walked away from this teacher summit in Chicago with 200 new heroes.

We have explored many facets of the project-based entrepreneurship educational experience throughout this book. But above all else, educators are the heart and soul of youth entrepreneurship education. Teachers are twenty-first century heroes, and their stories are heroic.

Let's delve into the real-life stories of NFTE founder Steve Mariotti, along with educators Ray Parris, Tara Coburn, and Obinno Coley, to shine a spotlight on their efforts.

---

224 "Hero," Merriam-Webster.

LIGHT EMERGES FROM DARKNESS[225]

On a sunny September Sunday in New York City in 1981, twenty-seven-year-old Steve Mariotti decided to go for a jog along the East River. He had been a high school state wrestling champion in Flint, Michigan where he grew up, and running was a nice way for him to stay in shape and clear his mind. But something would happen on this afternoon that would change the course of Mariotti's life forever.

A year and a half earlier, Mariotti had reached a low point in his young life. Growing up, his dream was to be an executive in the automotive business. Despite a difficult struggle with dyslexia, Mariotti had found creative workarounds to achieve academic success.

By age twenty-five, it looked like Mariotti was on his way to fulfilling his career dream. Upon completing his M.B.A. from the University of Michigan, he landed a highly selective position at Ford Motor Company as a financial analyst. He got off to a great start, impressing senior leadership with his financial acumen and strategic insights.

But an incident involving Mariotti speaking up about Ford's business practices in apartheid South Africa was not well received. Mariotti felt that Ford should reform its business operations in South Africa where the white minority government was brutally oppressing the black majority, some of whom were working at a Ford plant in the country.

---

225 Mariotti and Devi, *Goodbye Homeboy: How My Students Drove Me Crazy and Inspired a Movement,* chap. 1-17.

Mariotti made it clear through numerous internal memos that Ford was complicit in this oppression if it allowed black employees at its plant to be mistreated. His opinion was deemed too controversial at the time, and he was fired.

Ultimately, Ford pulled out of South Africa under intense pressure from activist groups, and Mariotti felt vindicated in standing firm against this injustice. His mother was a renowned special education teacher in Michigan, and she had taught her son to speak up when something was not right.

To this day, Mariotti has no regrets about shining a spotlight on the brutal mistreatment of black workers in South Africa and he would do the same again regardless of the consequences. But his reputation had been tarnished by his managers at Ford upon his exit. An invitation to come back to work for the company he once loved was not forthcoming.

Mariotti's dream of a career in the automotive industry was entirely shattered. "Growing up outside of 'Motor City' in Michigan," Mariotti said, "the only industry I ever considered for my career was the automobile business."

Unfortunately, word had traveled fast about Mariotti's dismissal and no other car company in Michigan would even return his phone calls. So, at the age of twenty-six, he fled to New York City in search of an opportunity to start over.

Beginning anew in New York City was a challenge. But Mariotti began to find his way when some conversations he struck up on the streets of Queens led him to recognize an opportunity to be an import/export entrepreneur.

He decided to focus on women's shoes since he remembered his mother talking facetiously about how women always seemed to want a new pair of shoes. By importing shoe products from Southeast Asia and enhancing their design, Mariotti figured he could market them as luxury products to retailers in the city and earn a healthy profit.

Through investing the small amount of money saved from his short stint at Ford, Mariotti established his own company. His business began to pick up quickly, and soon he was selling hundreds of thousands of dollars of shoes per month. Mariotti felt a tremendous sense of empowerment in creating his own venture and life was back on track, or so he thought.

Things took a dramatic turn when he set out for his run along the East River on that fateful Sunday afternoon in September of 1981. Just as he reached the walkway along the river with glorious views of the Brooklyn Bridge, a group of young teenagers grabbed him from behind, forced his arms behind his back and demanded his money. In shock, Mariotti broke free and began to run for his life down the path.

They caught up to him, though, this time securing him by holding knives up to his throat. One punched him in the gut. Another shoved him and threatened to slice him unless he gave up his money. Shaking and with tears rolling down his face, Mariotti grabbed the only money he had, a $10 bill in his running shorts, and handed it to them.

They then forcefully picked him up and dangled him over the edge of the fencing along the river, threatening to drown him.

Suddenly, one of the boys signaled that it was time to go, and the others brought him down off the fence and left the scene.

The incident ended and Mariotti was physically unharmed. But in the ensuing days, he had lost his ability to sleep due to intense anxiety.

Every time he began to drift off in the evening to fall asleep, he would suddenly wake up in a panic sweating profusely. Mariotti sank into a deep and uncontrollable depression.

After months of insomnia and sickness resulting from his depleted immune system, Mariotti was diagnosed with post-traumatic stress disorder (PTSD). His doctor suggested that Mariotti confront his fears by taking them head on. Recalling his mother's experience as a special education teacher focused on disadvantaged high school students, Mariotti decided to completely switch gears with his career again and go into teaching.

"Perhaps I took my doctor's advice too literally," Mariotti said jokingly, "but somehow I felt compelled to follow in my mom's footsteps as I tried to pull myself out of the darkness of my depression." Gathering himself with every ounce of courage he could muster, Mariotti set out to invest his energy into helping the same kinds of kids that had mugged him.

* * *

Mariotti's transition into teaching was anything but easy, though. His first position was at the most crime-ridden and lowest-performing school in the state of New York at the time—the Boys and Girls High School in Brooklyn.

The state had gathered evidence indicating that students who graduated from high school had higher incomes, longer life expectancy, and lower levels of crime compared to dropouts. Mariotti's assignment was to teach math to the most disadvantaged students at this high school with the aim of trying to help them graduate.

A year into his new teaching career, however, it was clear that Mariotti was having no impact in trying to inspire his kids to stay in school. His students were unmotivated, unruly, and unkind. They treated him like he was the child, locking him out of the classroom on numerous occasions and telling him to quit teaching because he had no talent.

On many days, Mariotti would think back to his mugging on the East River. He wondered why he had decided to jump into the classroom with the same sorts of kids that had sent him into a devastating depression.

Mariotti surmised that his students weren't responding to him because the approach used in the math textbooks was not put in the context of their actual lives. They could not see how the material was relevant to any part of their lives, so they simply shut off. As he thought about this disconnect, he became even more determined to identify new ways to motivate his kids to graduate.

He needed success with these students not only because he wanted to help them, but because this was his only path to overcome the anguish resulting from the mugging incident. Besides, he could not afford another flame out in his career like what had happened back home in Michigan at Ford. Quitting was not an option.

One day, Mariotti decided to try a different approach by getting feedback directly from his students on what they thought he should do to help them. Mariotti invited them for some free pizza after school to have an informal discussion about how he could improve his teaching. During this gathering, Mariotti's students told him that the only thing they ever found interesting in his class was when he shared his experiences as an entrepreneur in New York City.

As the chatter grew louder and the pizza was nearly gone, one student named Ed Blanding raised his hand. Ed was perpetually disengaged in class and had never spoken up before. To Mariotti's amazement, Blanding proceeded to recite the entire profit and loss statement from his import/export business as if it was his own business.

Mariotti was stunned. Here was a kid who was completely inattentive in class and on the verge of dropping out, yet he had retained in depth concepts about business like he was an M.B.A. student. Blanding had articulated this off the top of his head without any preparation.

In that moment, a light bulb turned on for Mariotti. He would use entrepreneurship as a vehicle through which to teach his students in a manner that motivated them to learn.

Mariotti began his next class by taking off his watch and asking his kids to name a price for which they could sell it. Several kids literally jumped out of their chairs to respond.

Others shouted prices with a level of enthusiasm unlike any he had seen before in a classroom.

He organized the class into buyers and sellers and asked them to present their pitches and negotiate a final price. These kids who had been entirely withdrawn and on track to drop out from school were smiling from ear to hear and finally showing an interest in learning.

He had found a way to break through and he could feel that he was on to something big. "There was this amazing insight that came from experimenting with entrepreneurship education in my high school classrooms," Mariotti revealed. "It became clear that this was a way to unlock the creative energy in my students." Empowered by his newfound realization, he trialed the new methods in classroom after classroom in the subsequent years, and the results were always the same.

Mariotti had found his calling. He would make entrepreneurship education for young people who needed it most his life's mission.

A few years later in 1987, Mariotti formed a nonprofit organization called the Network for Teaching Entrepreneurship. Corporate donations poured in and schools jumped on board as they saw the program's influence on students. Over 1 million students have now had their lives impacted by the insight Mariotti had as a high school educator in Brooklyn in the 1980s. [226,227]

---

226 "Preparing The Next Generation – 2018 Annual Report."

227 Mariotti and Devi, *Goodbye Homeboy,* preface.

From Steve Mariotti's darkest moments, light now shines brightly.

FROM TRAGEDY TO TRANSFORMING MINDSETS

Traveling thousands of miles across the Atlantic Ocean, Hurricane Hugo ripped through the U.S. Virgin Islands with devastating force on September 17, 1989.[228]

Prisons were destroyed, and violent criminals ran free. Schools and homes were demolished. Grocery stores were wiped out. Power and water supplies were cut off. The people of the U.S. Virgin Islands lost nearly everything and were in a state of desperation as the aftermath set in.

Fifteen-year-old Ray Parris was no stranger to tragedy when Hugo hit his native island of St. Croix, one of the U.S. Virgin Islands. Just a year earlier, his father had been viciously murdered by members of a drug gang that had established itself on the island. Parris's mother had pleaded with his father to stay focused on the family grocery store as their means to earn a living.

But his father began using drugs and chose to join the gang to earn some fast money. Ultimately, a dispute over drug payments that Parris's father apparently owed the gang led to his death.

Parris recalls one specific incident prior to his father's murder that will stay with him forever. Some leaders of the gang

---

228 "Hurricane Hugo."

had brought Parris's father back home after an argument in the streets.

They forcefully slammed his dad up against the front door of the family house. His father screamed to be let in, but Parris refused to open the door.

"I was sure the gang was going to kill my mom, my brother, my sisters, and me along with my dad if I let them in," Parris recalled. "I was overcome with fear, but I held that door closed with every ounce of energy in my fourteen-year old body," he continued. Eventually, he could no longer resist the strength of the three grown men holding his father captive, and they crashed through the door.

A man from the gang then held a gun to Parris's father's head. Just as he was about to pull the trigger, they recognized Parris as the young artist who sold beautifully spray-painted t-shirts and custom designer clothing at their family grocery store. They told Parris's father that they would spare his life that night because of the magnificent clothing Parris had designed for them.

But Parris knew how the gang operated from overhearing conversations of members that frequented the family store. When someone didn't pay them, it was only a matter of time before that person would be dead. Just a few weeks after the incident at the front door of Parris's family home, his father was brutally murdered.

The circumstances of Parris's father's death in 1988, followed by the absolute devastation of Hurricane Hugo in 1989, would be enough to break the spirit of most teenagers. But Parris was not an ordinary young man.

Parris had developed an ability to view even the most difficult circumstances as opportunities for personal growth. "My mom used to say that the measure of my character was found not in how I handle the good moments, but how I fight through the tough times," Parris said. Moreover, he had a natural gift for creativity through art, which had become his escape from the hardships he faced.

After Hurricane Hugo, Parris's mother made the very emotional decision to put him on a plane to go live with his uncle in Miami, so he could attend an art school in the city. "My mother is my hero," he proclaimed. "She made the most selfless decision a mother could ever make in kissing me goodbye, so I could pursue a better life." Parris helped to refurbish the family grocery store so his mother could get back on her feet, then he was on his way to Florida.

Parris was fortunate that his talent for artistic design and his entrepreneurial drive were recognized by his uncle who helped him enroll in the New World School of Arts in Miami. There, he experienced a very different environment than the one he grew up with in St. Croix. Teachers at New World focused on cultivating his artistic talents and molding his ethos to think about applying his abilities to career opportunities.

"New World literally changed my life," Parris said, "for the first time, I began to see that I could combine my passion for art with my burgeoning interest in entrepreneurship to build a career."

After New World, Parris went on to earn a Master's in fine arts and education at the Maryland Institute College of Art (MICA). To pay his way through school, Parris founded his own record label and graphic design company called Parafruit. This enabled him to sell albums and design services to students at MICA and other local universities.

As Parafruit's profits took off and Parris worked his way through college, he started to think about how he could have a positive impact in his community. He became increasingly aware that without the selflessness of his mom, the support of his uncle in Miami, and the extraordinary educational opportunities he had at New World and MICA, his life would have turned out very differently.

"I probably would have ended up selling drugs and perhaps even be dead back home without my mom, my uncle, and my teachers," Parris said, "and through this realization, I began to discover that my calling would be to share with others how art and entrepreneurship re-shaped my life so that I could change the trajectories of other young lives."

Fast forward to the present day, Parris is one of the most inspiring, innovative, and decorated teachers Miami has ever known. In 2012, he received a proclamation from the School Board of Miami-Dade County for helping youth in the Liberty City area of Miami through his non-profit, Parafruit Education, established for students to develop skills in multi-media, fine arts, and entrepreneurship.

In 2014, he was named the Global Enterprising Educator of the Year by NFTE. In 2018, through NFTE's Model Teacher

Challenge,[229] Parris was named National Teacher of the Year[230] for his work in and out of the classroom to advance both students' and fellow teachers' entrepreneurial skills and opportunities.

Recently, he was named Miami-Dade County's 2020 Francisco R. Walker Teacher of the Year Runner-up.[231] He currently serves as the Department head of Digital Media and Entrepreneurship at Hialeah Miami-Lakes Senior High School (HML), where he teaches STEM and entrepreneurship classes to students in grades nine through twelve.

Based on his experience as an educator, Parris has come to believe all young people have an innate ability to be creative and think like an entrepreneur. But too often, this creative spirit is not recognized or cultivated in a way that helps young people identify their own unique path to contribute to our economy and society. Parris said the result is that too many young people end up turning their back on a world they believe turns its back on them.

"The beauty of teaching entrepreneurship to my students is that it's never about me," Parris explained. "It's about pushing my students to discover what interests them and then using my experience to coach them through the process of turning that into a product or service that has real value." A central part of his focus as an educator is on building the eight domains

---

229 "Recognition and Leadership Opportunities."

230 "Miami Educator Wins Cash Prize in NFTE Model Teacher Challenge."

231 Colleen Wright, "'You have to love what you do.' Meet Miami-Dade's four teacher of the year finalists."

of the Entrepreneurial Mindset in his students so they are prepared to flourish in the twenty-first century.

In overcoming the personal tragedies of his youth and transforming his life through art and entrepreneurship, Ray Parris is demonstrating to young people every day how they, too, can overcome whatever obstacles life may throw their way.

LEARNING THE HARD WAY

Tara Coburn learned the hard way what it's like to face the accelerating pace of automation in the twenty-first century.

Growing up as the daughter of a high school English and business teacher in San Jose, California, Coburn decided to major in English at San Jose State University. In order to pay for school, she got a job as an administrative assistant at The Travel Shoppe in Los Gatos, California.

She had originally planned to follow in her mother's footsteps and be a teacher. But through her position at the Travel Shoppe, she developed a passion for business and the travel industry. As her interest grew, she began to set her sights on a career in this field. However, her new career dream would not come to fruition as she had envisioned.

After graduating from San Jose State with an English degree in 2003, Coburn was promoted to head of operations overseeing three retail travel locations and thirty-five independent contractors. In just three years, she had gone from part-time administrative assistant to being responsible for the end-to-end operations of a thriving travel agency.

"The path to becoming a successful businesswoman was clear, and I was certain that I was on my way," she said. Her plan was to learn all she could from the founder of The Travel Shoppe, and then start her own business when she was ready. But something unexpected happened just as she started to feel like her dream was within reach.

It was called the internet.

The travel agency business was one of the first industries to be upended by the internet in the early part of the twenty-first century. Websites like Expedia made it easier and faster to search for and book travel online, so many consumers abandoned travel agencies in favor of self-service travel planning online.[232]

Coupled with the post 9-11 decision by airlines to end travel agent commissions on air sales, this caused a massive shift in the industry. Coburn began to re-think her plan to become a travel business owner.

Fortunately, when the travel agency door closed, another one opened. Oak Grove High School in San Jose, where her mother Joyce Coburn had taught since 1969, had an opening for an English teacher. She quickly obtained the required credentials and got the job. In November 2004, Coburn began her new career as an educator.

It didn't take long, however, before she realized that what she was teaching to students in her English classes wasn't exactly

---

232 Suzanne Bearn, "How technology has transformed the travel industry."

what they needed to know to prosper in the twenty-first century. "Even though I love Shakespeare, I just didn't see how a student's ability to interpret and understand him had any impact on their future success," declared Coburn.

She took a critical look at the curriculum she was teaching, and she began to question its relevance to her students' futures. As a result, she began to develop a more real-world based curriculum for her English classes—one where students learned transferable skills, such as clear and effective communication, that would help them to be successful both in college and in the workplace.

After several years teaching what she called "applied English," she received a wonderful opportunity. Her mother retired from teaching, and Coburn became the new director of two fantastic programs her mother founded at Oak Grove: The Academy of Hospitality & Tourism and The Academy of Business & Finance.

Through this transition, Coburn found her calling. Both programs focused on teaching at-risk youth workplace skills while they were still in high school. Students entered during their sophomore year and stayed together as a small learning community supported by Coburn and her core teachers for three years.

It was a few years after taking over these programs that Coburn discovered NFTE. "For me, project-based entrepreneurship education was a perfect fit. It completely aligned with my values and beliefs when it came to educating youth," revealed Coburn. She took to the curriculum quickly and saw great results with her students.

Students who were previously disengaged with school became engaged in meaningful real-world projects. She watched students' confidence in communicating and problem-solving grow. She helped them create and start their own companies, and then saw them turn around and help their parents with actual home-based businesses.

"Teaching the Entrepreneurial Mindset to students changed my life," Coburn stated emphatically. "It altered how I create lessons and educational experiences for students. It brought validity to the skills-based curriculum that I had developed, and it showed me that I was also an entrepreneur."

Today, Coburn supports NFTE's Bay Area teachers as a Master Educator, the highest level that an NFTE educator can attain. She also assists her fellow Career Technical Education teachers at East Side Union High School District as a teacher-leader and consultant.

Most importantly, she is doing exactly what she taught her students to do: find and follow their passions. For her, this means coming out of the classroom to become a motivational speaker and life coach for teens in addition to her other responsibilities.

"Through my experiences with NFTE, I have come to realize that my purpose is to help support youth in discovering their passions and aligning themselves with future success," Coburn said.

She went on to explain that she would like to see more schools adopt project-based entrepreneurship education because it takes students out of their comfort zones. Doing so helps young people see that finding their own unique path to prosperity is a process, and that every step they take to explore new horizons is helping them to discover who they were meant to be.

Although Coburn had to learn the hard way about the impact of automation in the twenty-first century, she is grateful that she discovered her own purpose through youth entrepreneurship education.

FINDING PURPOSE IN DEVELOPING YOUNG MINDSETS

Obinno Coley fell to his knees with tears rolling down his face.

Alone on Christmas Eve morning in the bedroom of his mother's house, he reached his arms up toward the sky and cried aloud for God to help him pull his life back together. He turned to the mirror sitting on the wall alongside him and was overcome with sadness. Coley was twenty-three years old and the father of two kids, but he had no money to buy them even a small gift for Christmas.

This was crushing him.

Coley had been living a lifestyle full of partying and night clubs, leaving his girlfriend to fend for herself. It hit Coley like a ton of bricks on that cold and snowy Christmas Eve of 2003 in Chicago that the status quo was unacceptable. He knew he must redirect his life to focus on serving others and providing for his family instead of being concerned solely with himself.

Five years earlier, Coley was feeling on top of the world as his football team at Evanston Township High School just outside of Chicago had an undefeated season. He was not the star of the team, but he played an important role as a starting cornerback on defense. In addition to football, he had spent countless hours studying in order to fulfill his dream of being the first one in his family to graduate from college.

Although he was just 5'9," 150 pounds and had just one interception his senior year, Coley was determined to earn a scholarship to play football in college. He created a highlight video of his best plays on the field and sent it to every university in the state of Illinois that had a team.

Few responded, but one Sunday afternoon shortly after the season ended, he got a call from a recruiter at Eastern Illinois University. They had one scholarship left and they were looking for a cornerback.

Coley jumped in the car with his mother the next day and drove three hours south down I-57 from Evanston to Charleston, IL to meet with the coaching staff. They liked what they saw and offered Coley a full scholarship on the spot.

"My mom screamed with joy so loudly that we could hear an echo across the campus," he said. The sacrifices that Coley's parents had made in moving him to the U.S. from Jamaica at age four in search of a better life had paid off. Coley had made his parents proud and he was overcome with emotion, too.

Coley spent the next four years playing football at Eastern Illinois, where he met his girlfriend Kim. She was a bright and caring young woman from St. Louis who was also looking to be the first in her family to graduate from college.

Their bond grew quickly and soon they had a child together. Coley had also fathered a child with a different woman prior to getting to know Kim. So, as a young university student and athlete, he had two children to look after.

Coley knew that he was not able to be the father he wanted to be during this time, but he was dependent on his scholarship financially, and he was resolute in his mission to graduate from Eastern in four years. In the spring of 2002, at the age of twenty-one, Coley did just that.

In the absence of football and the structure of school, however, Coley rapidly became disoriented after graduation. He didn't have much work experience because he had been busy playing football, studying, and being with Kim and their son when he could. Coley moved back in with his mom in Chicago in the summer of 2002 and Kim moved home to St. Louis to live with her parents.

The next nine months of Coley's life were a blur of juggling entry-level jobs and spending everything he earned on drinking, nightclubs, and courting women. On some evenings, he felt great. But he would then wake up the next morning feeling depressed about being away from Kim and their son.

This cycle of excessive late nights followed by early morning regrets is what ultimately led him to fall to his knees in tears on the morning of Christmas Eve of 2003. "I knew right then and there that I had to make a change," Coley said. Turning to his faith, he could sense that God was leading him to move to St. Louis to be with Kim, their son, and Kim's family.

Arriving in St. Louis, Coley found a job selling financial services, and he had a very successful run in business over the next decade. He felt immense pride in being able to provide for his family and there were no more Christmases without gifts.

Coley had also gotten himself away from the temptations of nightlife in Chicago that had brought him down. But he still felt as if there was something missing in his life.

During this same period in St. Louis, Coley had also been attending Bond Avenue Church where he volunteered to teach Sunday school. With each passing year, he could see through this experience that he had a gift for impacting young people.

"I taught Sunday school in St. Louis for eight years without realizing that God was preparing me for what would ultimately become my life's work to serve others," Coley said. God's plan for Coley's life would soon be revealed.

Coley went back to school to get his master's degree in education from Missouri Baptist University. On the first day of his student-teacher assignment that was part of his master's program, the wife of his host teacher at McCluer High School in St. Louis went into labor. Coley had been expecting an easy orientation into the teaching profession, but this obviously would not be the case.

Explaining that he had to run to the hospital to be with his wife, Coley's host teacher rushed out of the classroom and handed him a text-book. The book had the word "Entrepreneurship" on the cover in big blue letters.

Coley opened the book to try to prepare himself to enter the classroom of twenty student's waiting for the day's lesson. An ordinary student-teacher would have buckled under the pressure. But Coley is anything but ordinary.

Instead of panicking, a feeling of serenity overcame Coley as he thumbed through the textbook. "In that moment, I could see the hand of God directing me to combine my passions for business, teaching, and uplifting young people. Entrepreneurship education would enable me to bring it all together," Coley said. Drawing on his experience from teaching Sunday school for eight years, he walked into the classroom and nailed the lesson plan.

And sure enough, Coley began to pursue his new passion of teaching entrepreneurship to young people with the same intensity he used to have for playing football. For his first full-time assignment, he chose Normandy High School, perhaps the most challenging school in all of St. Louis.

The school had been taken over by the state due to severe under-performance, having scored just 12 on a scale of 140 that Missouri uses to measure student outcomes. The new principle wanted to try something fresh and he thought maybe Coley could make a difference.

Five years later, Normandy High School had been transformed, scoring a 90 out of 140 on the state scale. A key element of the turnaround, of course, has been the project-based entrepreneurship education curriculum led by Coley.

He shared dozens of examples of how he has worked to ignite the Entrepreneurial Mindset in his students as they build business plans based on their own ideas. Moreover, once students could see how math, science, and English applied to the real-world businesses they were creating, they began to focus on those subjects more vigorously.

In recognition of his accomplishments, Coley was honored as a Global Enterprising Educator in 2018 by NFTE.[233] And today, he is known as the champion of entrepreneurship education in St. Louis. In 2019, he became an NFTE Master Educator and he has been instrumental in helping the non-profit grow from just one school in St. Louis to eight.

In elevating his role to Master Educator, Coley aims to reach 600 under-resourced students per year in the St. Louis metro area by recruiting and training additional teachers. And from there, the sky is the limit.

He closed our discussion with a football analogy. Coley said, "You know what Tom Brady said on *60 Minutes* when he was asked which of his Super Bowl rings is the best one? He said, 'The best Super Bowl ring is the next one.'"[234]

This is the kind of inspiration that Obinno Coley brings to his students every day in St. Louis through youth entrepreneurship education.

---

233 "Coley Selected as 2018 Global Enterprising Educator."

234 60 Minutes, "Tom Brady's favorite Super Bowl ring? 'The next one.'"

CONCLUSION

The real-life stories of Steve Mariotti, Ray Parris, Tara Coburn, and Obinno Coley highlight the heroic role that educators play in altering the trajectories of young people's lives through project-based entrepreneurship education. Based on the evidence set forth throughout this book, I would argue that imparting the Entrepreneurial Mindset in young people through entrepreneurship education is one of the most impactful professions of the twenty-first century.

CHAPTER 10

ENTREPRENEURSHIP EDUCATION FOR ALL

———

Computer Science for All.[235]

This is the name of a national initiative to make Computer Science (CS) education available to all K-12 students across the U.S. The imperative to teach coding skills in classrooms is one of the most significant education reform movements of the twenty-first century. The program, officially launched at the White House in early 2016, places a special emphasis on under-resourced communities.

CS for All makes perfect sense given the central role that STEM disciplines play in our modern economy. It is inspiring to see federal, state, and local government officials coming together, along with nonprofits and industry partners, to advance CS education in a such a material way.

However, as we have observed throughout this book, enhancing STEM education is not enough to equip young people for the Future of Work. In fact, a recent World Economic Forum report characterized the combination of STEM skills together with capacities such as creativity, collaboration, and communication as the "golden ticket" for the jobs of tomorrow.[236]

It is therefore vital that we think more holistically about educational programs aimed at workforce development, and at fostering the sort of ethos necessary for young people to become value creators in the twenty-first century. As such, we must move with a sense of urgency to ensure that young

---

235 "CS for All."

236 Anna Powers, "Davos Announces That The Highest Growth Careers Are In STEM, With A Caveat."

learners develop the Entrepreneurial Mindset through project-based entrepreneurship education.

Every student who reaches adulthood without the benefit of this educational experience is a missed opportunity for all of us. The time has come to launch a sister program to CS for All, one that has a complimentary mission to imbue the right-brain capacities that young learners must build alongside STEM skills.

Let's call this new imperative Entrepreneurship Education for All (Entrepreneurship for All for short).

A BIG HAIRY AUDACIOUS GOAL

Entrepreneurship for All is what Ruthe Farmer would call a BHAG—a Big Hairy Audacious Goal.[237]

Farmer is the Chief Evangelist for CSforALL,[238] a nonprofit that brings educators, administrators, school boards, state education departments, researchers, and the private sector together to facilitate CS education for K-12 students. She is one of the country's foremost experts on incubating and scaling new topics into our U.S. educational systems.

Growing up on the west coast of the U.S., Farmer moved sixty-eight times during her childhood. Consequently, she did not have the benefit of a linear progression in her math

237 Collins and Porras, *Built to Last: Successful Habits of Visionary Companies,* 9.

238 "Join the Movement to Bring Computer Science to ALL Students."

education. In college, Farmer took a course on women's studies and realized another gap in her K-12 education was not learning about the important role that women have played in U.S. history.

These two deficiencies in her early education drove Farmer to take on tech and engineering education as her own personal BHAG, with a special emphasis on preparing more women for careers in tech. Based on Farmer's extraordinary achievements, she was honored at the White House in 2013 as a "Champion of Change" for Tech Inclusion.[239]

Farmer's turning point came in 2001 when she landed a position as a program manager for Girl Scouts-Columbia River Council (now Girl Scouts of Oregon and SW Washington). Intel had recently awarded the national nonprofit with a grant to help grow the pipeline of engineering-educated young women entering the workforce, and the Girl Scouts-Columbia River Council was among the cohorts chosen to pilot the effort. Council leadership had planned to hire an external contractor to implement the program, but Farmer stepped in and convinced management that she could lead the effort herself.

In collaboration with Girl Scouts of the USA and Intel, Farmer helped design a curriculum that would later be called Design and Discovery.[240] The initiative brought girl scouts together in teams for design-thinking sessions to work through engineering solutions to problems identified by the girls-from

239 The Obama Whitehouse, "Champions of Change: Tech Inclusion."
240 "Design and Discovery."

product conception, to development, prototyping, testing, and marketing. The projects were then presented at feeder fairs for the Intel International Science and Engineering Fair (ISEF), the largest international science and engineering competition for K-12 students in the world.[241]

"The program was a breakthrough success," Farmer said, "and it was eventually implemented in over sixty Girl Scout councils in the U.S. It even made its way into the school system in Ireland."

The initiative received wide acclaim from Intel, Girl Scout leadership, and business leaders. As a testament to the program's impact, it is still in use today. Through her work at Girl Scouts, Farmer had found her calling.

She went on to earn her M.B.A. from Oxford University where she studied social entrepreneurship, with a concentration in incubating and scaling innovative new topics into educational systems. Following a nine-year stint leading strategy and launching K-16 programs at the National Center for Women & Information Technology (NCWIT), Farmer landed a position at the White House as Senior Policy Advisor for Tech Inclusion, working on developing and implementing President Obama's CS for All initiative.

In 2017, Farmer joined the nonprofit organization CSforALL as Chief Evangelist, where her work to bring computing education to young people continues to the present day.

---

241 "Intel International Science and Engineering Fair."

As evidence of the success of the unique collective impact effort of CS for All more broadly, today forty-seven U.S. states have adopted education policies that allow CS course work to count toward core high school graduation requirements.[242] This is up from just twenty-eight states in 2017.[243]

Furthermore, nine out of every ten parents surveyed express a desire for CS to be taught in their local K-12 school districts.[244] When Farmer first started as an advocate for technology education nearly two decades ago, the topic barely registered.

Entrepreneurship for All is effectively where the CS for All movement was twenty years ago. It is our Big Hairy Audacious Goal.

The percentage of parents, teachers, administrators, and school board leaders that think of entrepreneurship as a topic that should be prioritized in secondary education is far lower than it should be. A big part of this gap is awareness. Some are simply not familiar with the concept of teaching entrepreneurship in the classroom to middle and high school students.

Too few have attended a youth entrepreneurship competition, mentored students through their business planning projects, or witnessed the energy in a classroom when young learners are empowered to turn their ideas into real business plans. And

242 "2019 State of Computer Science Education: Equity and Diversity."

243 Ibid.

244 Cynthia English, "Parents, Students Want Computer Science Education in School."

many have not fully grasped how much more capable today's digitally native students are at cultivating innovative solutions to real-world problems compared to prior generations.

Most importantly, very few have crystallized the linkage between youth entrepreneurship education and the mindset requirements for the twenty-first century economy.

But this must change. The Future of Work demands it.

The CS for All vanguard is the best example of what it will take to bring Entrepreneurship for All to life. Hence, I asked Farmer to work together with me to devise some guiding principles to consider as we embark upon this new journey together.

Farmer and I codified seven core tenets as outlined below.

TENET ONE: THE UNIT OF CHANGE IS LOCAL

In our U.S. secondary educational systems (middle and high school levels for ages eleven to eighteen), there are approximately 30,000 local units of change broken down as follows:

- 14,000 public-school Districts[245]

- 13,000 private schools[246]

- 3,000 charter schools[247]

---

245 National Center for Education Statistics (Table 214.10).

246 Ibid.

247 "Key Facts About Charter Schools."

Moreover, there are over 100,000 individuals overseeing education policy at these local levels, including over 90,000 looking after public-school Districts.[248] As a result, Farmer described the U.S. as having "probably the most complex and distributed secondary educational systems in the world."

Other governments have the power to enact national changes through one conversation, but our hyper-local U.S. systems prevent that. Here is what Farmer had to say about how difficult it has been to initiate and scale Computer Science for All in this environment:

> *Korea just made it a requirement for software engineering for all its students. We can't do that. No one in this country, not even the President, can say you must teach computer science. So, it must be done at a grassroots level by individual people.*[249]

It is clear, then, that Entrepreneurship for All isn't going to happen in the U.S. through a top down mandate. Even if the federal government set aside billions in funding tomorrow to implement the initiative, decisions must still be made by local school boards, administrators, and educators. Moreover, if ownership is not transferred to school principals and teachers in an authentic way that aligns with their own local school objectives and community values, the full benefits of the programming cannot be realized.[250]

---

248 "About Us."

249 Nation of Makers, "NOMCON 2018 Keynote: Ruthe Farmer."

250 Cynthia Coburn, "Rethinking Scale: Moving Beyond Numbers to Deep and Lasting Change," 3.

Local education policy makers must consciously decide to implement project-based entrepreneurship education, otherwise it simply won't happen. And these decisions need to be made in the context of a full portfolio of required curricula and a wide range of competing interests lobbying to have one topic or another brought into classrooms. Even decisions about after school and summer school programming are made mostly at the local level.

It is important to point out that each individual local unit of change is distinct. This is by no means a one-size-fits-all secondary educational system in the U.S.

As such, it is critical to understand the people, priorities, culture, geographical constraints and other considerations of each District and school in order to position the Entrepreneurship for All movement within the uniqueness of each environment. And a sizable emphasis must be placed on serving under-resourced communities, where the need is most acute.

Further, the initiative itself must be highly flexible and adaptable to accommodate wide-ranging diversity. We have seen Districts such as Miami-Dade and Broward counties in Florida, East Side Union and L.A. Unified in California, and Normandy Schools Collaborative in St. Louis lead the way in this regard.

A great way to begin our grass roots campaign for Entrepreneurship for All at the local level would be to provide a copy of this book to every school board member, administrator and teacher across all our 30,000 local units of change in the U.S. And let's include staff members too!

Contact information for your local school District board members can be obtained through the National School Boards Association (www.nsba.org),[251] a nonprofit based in Alexandria, Virginia. A list of public-school Districts, and website links arranged by state in alphabetical order, is available through Ballotpedia (www.ballotpedia.org).[252] You can also find contact information for your local school board members, administrators, staff members, and teachers from your local school District website or school website.

The unit of change is local; this is our first organizing principle for bringing Entrepreneurship for All to fruition.

TENET TWO: TEACHERS ARE HEROES, AND EVANGELISTS TOO

The second precept we devised involves educators. Even more localized than the unit of change at the school District level is our teachers, who interact with students every day in classrooms. This is of course where tangible impact occurs.

When educators are passionate about their teaching method, and when student engagement is high, a level of energy is unlocked that inspires a thirst to go beyond. How do we bring scale and sustainability to this sort of high-impact interaction between teachers and students?

Northwestern University School of Education professor Cynthia Coburn wrote about the necessary ingredients for

---

251 "About Us."

252 "United States school districts."

bringing scale to reforms in K-12 education in a research paper entitled *Rethinking Scale: Moving Beyond Numbers to Deep and Lasting Change* as follows:

> *...reforms must effect deep and consequential change in classroom practice...that goes beyond surface structures or procedures (such as changes in materials, classroom organization, or the addition of specific activities) to alter teachers' beliefs, norms of social interaction, and pedagogical principles as enacted in the curriculum. By teachers' beliefs, I am referring to teachers' underlying assumptions about how students learn, the nature of subject matter, expectations for students, or what constitutes effective instruction.*[253]

This is precisely the sort of substantive change we see every day with educators embracing the Entrepreneurship Pathway pedagogy. Project-based entrepreneurship education deeply and consequentially changes the basic nature of these classrooms. Teachers' belief systems reflect their truth that they can instill the Entrepreneurial Mindset and change the trajectories of their students' lives by embracing a fundamentally different learning method.

On a personal note, prior to the teacher summit in Chicago in 2019 which I referenced in Chapter 9, I had some doubt about whether I could summon the will to complete this book given my other personal and professional responsibilities.

---

253 Cynthia Coburn, "Rethinking Scale: Moving Beyond Numbers to Deep and Lasting Change." 3.

First-time authors often struggle mightily to finish books they start.[254] But when I witnessed up close the zeal with which these educators shared story after story about how teaching the Entrepreneurial Mindset transformed the lives of their students, I felt a renewed sense of vigor that carried me through the process.

NFTE teachers are some of the most inspiring and dedicated twenty-first century heroes that you will ever find. I cannot imagine a cohort that is better equipped to uphold and evangelize the merits of youth entrepreneurship education.

Our second tenet for seeding the Entrepreneurship for All movement is galvanizing a core group of educators that can speak to the impact they are having on students. I am thrilled to report that this is an area where the movement is already way ahead of the curve.

TENET THREE: PARENTS HAVE POWERFUL VOICES

When Farmer thinks back to her early years of attempting to get CS for All on the radar, she recalls that a critical step was grassroots efforts to get parents to understand the importance of CS education for their kids. Once parents began to see how critical it was for their children to learn coding skills to thrive in the twenty-first century, their voices became a powerful force in influencing school boards to adapt their curricula accordingly.

"The early years of CS for All were all about stimulating demand at the local level," Farmer recounted. "Parents are

---

254 Joe Bunting, "Why You Can't Finish Writing Your Book."

the single most potent advocacy group when it comes to influencing education policy locally." Farmer went on to explain that getting parents, along with grandparents and other family members, to see how critical project-based entrepreneurship education is to prepare young people for the Future of Work will be vital in getting the movement off the ground.

Perhaps the measurement for success can be similar to how the CS for All initiative quantifies it, by using survey benchmarks. When nine out of ten parents indicate a desire for their children to have access to entrepreneurship education in their middle and high school classrooms, we will have reached a tipping point in bringing scale to Entrepreneurship for All.

So, how can we work toward achieving this benchmark? Here are a few steps that can be taken immediately:

1. Purchase copies of this book and provide them to parents, grandparents, or other concerned citizens that may be interested in advancing the cause. 100% of the proceeds from this book are charitable contributions to NFTE. As such, advocating for the movement in this way both supports NFTE's mission directly, and it accelerates Entrepreneurship for All at the same time.

2. Recommend that parents find out if project-based entrepreneurship is available in their local middle and high schools. If not, suggest that they contact their local school board members to urge that this topic be put on the priority list for consideration, either for stand-alone implementation or through combination

within existing courses. Importantly, emphasize that the Future of Work is the imperative that makes this change so urgent.

3. Recommend that parents, grandparents, and other family members attend a local or regional youth entrepreneurship competition run by NFTE or other similar organizations.[255] There is nothing more compelling than experiencing a competition in person to understand the effectiveness of this unique learning method.

4. Persuade parents, grandparents, and other family members to get involved as mentors to help coach students through their business planning projects. Spending just one hour with a student in this capacity is another fantastic way to open people's eyes as to how meaningful the educational experience is for both students and mentors alike.

To reiterate, we must go beyond just helping parents understand the critical nature of youth entrepreneurship education. We need parents to take a step further by contacting their local school board members to request that this pedagogy be implemented in classrooms, with the dynamics shaping the Future of Work as the driving force behind the required transformation.

Magnifying the power of parental voices is our third tenet for hastening the Entrepreneurship for All vanguard.

---

255 Kayla Prochnow, "The Best Entrepreneurship Competitions for K-12 Students."

TENET FOUR: WHAT YOU COUNT, COUNTS

Next, Farmer revealed that when it comes to influencing education policy in the U.S. secondary educational systems, "what you count, counts."

For example, Farmer has observed that when surveys are distributed by the U.S. Department of Education, local school boards, administration, and educators take notice. They become especially aware of topics that are "on the radar screen" if questions appear for the first time in these surveys.

Farmer highlighted the Civil Rights Data Collection (CRDC) effort as one that is particularly significant.[256] A major thrust in support of CS for All has been getting the U.S. Department of Education to collect data on CS education in the bi-annual CRDC survey.

For the 2017-18 CRDC surveys, the department introduced four questions on the availability of CS in grades nine through twelve and participation of students by age, race, and gender. Now that CS is a topic that is being tracked at the federal level, Farmer hopes that school administrators will put more focus on accelerating CS education programs. In this way, schools can report back with a clear "yes" they have implemented or have plans to implement CS education.

Another critical way that "what you count, counts" regarding CS for All was the push to have CS coursework satisfy core graduation requirements, as opposed to being elective credit.

---

256 "Wide-Ranging Education Access And Equity Data Collected From Our Nation's Public Schools."

Once students learned they could take CS and have it count toward a math or science credit (and that it is no longer in competition with other elective courses like music, art, or theater), a significant expansion in the number of students enrolling in CS classes took place.

Farmer believes that the same idea of "what you count, counts" holds true for Entrepreneurship for All. Therefore, we made this our fourth tenet for proliferating project-based entrepreneurship education in our middle and high schools across the U.S.

TENET 5: STATE GOVERNORS AND DEPARTMENTS OF EDUCATION FOR U.S. STATES ARE KEY

State governors[257] and Departments of Education for U.S. States,[258] play a key role in setting and overseeing education policy. Overall, states provide about forty-seven percent of the funding for public K-12 education, with local funding accounting for around forty-five percent, and federal funding covering the remaining eight percent.[259] Our fifth proposition is identifying and fostering relationships with a handful of state governors and Departments of Education that are looking to bring innovation to K-12 schools, and working together with them to champion and evangelize the initiative.

"Governor Hutchinson from Arkansas and Governor Raimondo from Rhode Island are two outstanding examples of

---

257 Sargrad and Partelow, "11 Ways New Governors Can Lead on Education Through Executive Actions."

258 "State Boards of Education."

259 National Center for Education Statistics (Table 235.10).

innovative leaders that have led the CS for All charge in their respective states," Farmer revealed. She pointed out that these two dynamic leaders have not only driven the movement in their states, but they have worked tirelessly to evangelize CS for All with their fellow governors across the country.

"Peer to peer influence among governors is the highest impact way to spread the word for a movement like this across states," Farmer continued. She added that the key is finding the governor willing to be the first out of the gate with new programs. Most leaders prefer to see tangible results from other states to ensure that best practices are in place before they are willing to put their political capital behind a new idea.

Twice per year, in the winter and summer, the National Governors Association (NGA) hosts governors for in person meetings to discuss the crucial issues states face, including education policy.[260] These meetings include open plenary sessions and committee meetings, as well as closed-door private meetings for governors only. The NGA also holds multiple events throughout the year tailored to public policy issues such as education and economic development.

These forums can be great opportunities to showcase programs like Entrepreneurship for All. But, Farmer stressed that having an initial small group of innovative governors, along with the support of their state Departments of Education, are an absolute must in order for peer to peer influence to be effective.

---

260 "NGA Meetings."

The National Association of State Boards of Education (www.nasbe.org)[261] is an excellent resource for accessing information about each state board. These state departments, state department heads, and of course the governor of each state, are an essential constituency that must be cultivated for Entrepreneurship for All to reach its potential.

TENET 6: FEDERAL GOVERNMENT SUPPORT IS VITAL

In December of 2015, the U.S. federal government passed Every Student Succeeds Act (ESSA)[262] which governs K-12 public education policy. In a rare showing of U.S. government bi-partisan support, ESSA replaced its predecessor No Child Left Behind (NCLB) in the U.S. Senate by a margin of eighty-five to twelve.[263] As a general matter, ESSA puts more control over education policy into the hands of states and local school Districts, while the federal government maintains less influence as a result.[264]

One of the bill's signature features is its requirement that states deploy a multiple-measures system of accountability,[265] beyond just standardized testing. This stipulation is there for a reason. There is widespread dissatisfaction with the superfluous emphasis on judging students primarily by standardized tests, and this provision is a response to that criticism.[266]

---

261 "State Boards of Education."

262 "New education law shifts federal influence over public schools."

263 Ibid.

264 Ibid.

265 Anne O'Brien, "5 Ways ESSA Impacts Standardized Testing."

266 Ibid.

The use of these additional indicators provides an opening for innovative states and school Districts to build a more holistic approach for students, including investments in developing the Entrepreneurial Mindset through project-based entrepreneurship education. The door has therefore swung wide open for Entrepreneurship for All to take hold. The timing is right to seize the moment at the state and local level.

But the federal government can, and should, play a more meaningful role in advancing Entrepreneurship for All than just passing the baton to states and localities. Congress is one of the first places to start.

In fact, Congresswoman Grace Meng of Queens, New York has emerged as a pioneer in championing youth entrepreneurship education on Capitol Hill. Congresswoman Meng recently introduced the Twenty-first Century Youth Entrepreneurship Act, a bill that would enable federal ESEA and Perkins dollars to be used toward expanding entrepreneurship programs in K-12 public schools, libraries, community spaces, and community colleges.[267]

"Entrepreneurship kindles the spark of creativity and ingenuity that has been such a cornerstone of our economy," Congresswoman Meng said.[268]

This is a tremendous example of how Congress can help advance the youth entrepreneurship education movement. But there is much more that can be done in Washington, D.C.

---

267 "Congresswoman introduces 21st Century Youth Entrepreneurship Act following Global Entrepreneurship Week."

268 Ibid.

The U.S. Department of Education[269] and the U.S. Department of Labor[270] also have a significant ability to influence K-12 education policy nationally. They can provide thought leadership, research on requirements for workforce readiness, and incentive programs through grants that seed the adoption of project-based entrepreneurship education. In fact, a proposal has recently been introduced to merge the two agencies into a new U.S. Department of Education and the Workforce.[271]

Ultimately, we should galvanize our lobbying efforts across all relevant constituencies within the U.S. federal government. The aim here is to craft a national initiative with sponsorship across both the executive and legislative branches. If CS for All can rise to the level of a programmatic educational priority announced at the White House by the President of the United States, so can Entrepreneurship for All.

Our sixth creed for progressing Entrepreneurship for All is enlisting U.S. federal government support through a strategically crafted lobbying campaign.

TENET 7: IT TAKES AN ECOSYSTEM TO SCALE
Our final tenet is that it takes an entire ecosystem with an all-hands-on-deck approach to build a movement like Entrepreneurship for All.

---

269 "The Federal Role in Education."

270 "The U.S. Department of Education and the Workforce."

271 Ibid.

"No act is too small when you are trying to build a grassroots initiative like this," Farmer expounded. "You really have to cast a wide net, create a broad coalition of partners, and work together to define roles and responsibilities. And do your best to divide and conquer."

Farmer added one thing that could have been done better regarding CS for All, with the benefit of hindsight, is to be more intentional and strategic about formulating an ecosystem strategy at the outset. She compared the ecosystem approach that CS for All had in the early years to building a plane while trying to fly it at the same time. Farmer sees a unique opportunity for the Entrepreneurship for All movement to take the blueprints from CS for All and use them as both lessons learned and best practices that have been refined over the past two decades.

"You might want to consider creating a central advocacy group for Entrepreneurship for All like we did through our nonprofit organization CSforALL," Farmer said. "In this way, evangelism and coordination across all the various stakeholders can be managed efficiently."

She went on to summarize the functions that each of the stakeholders across the seven organizing principles play, in addition to the critical role that the private sector plays in funding programs, volunteering, offering apprenticeships, and ultimately being the source of employment for most of our young students. In the case of CSforALL, there are over 500 member organizations of all types partnering together to build local, regional, and national communities that collaborate to advance their collective mission.[272]

---

272 "Project and Programs: Member Directory."

Farmer and I discussed two more pertinent aspects of a comprehensive ecosystem for Entrepreneurship for All that are worth highlighting. These two additional components are related to international cooperation and higher education considerations.

International Cooperation

First, if the charter of the movement is both U.S. and ultimately global, it is useful to connect to what is going on in other parts of the world on the topic of youth entrepreneurship education. It turns out that thought leaders from around the world are similarly embracing this imperative to develop entrepreneurial thinking in young people in consideration of the Future of Work.

For instance, the European Commission has developed the Entrepreneurship Competence Framework which outlines a conceptual structure for entrepreneurship education across the EU.[273] A core component of this initiative is the Embedding Entrepreneurship Education (EEE) Teaching Toolkit, which consists of twenty-three modules that can be combined in various ways to create new academic courses or extend existing ones.[274]

Among EU countries, Finland stands out with its K-12 educational program that has been modernized using these teaching concepts. Preparing students for the twenty-first century is

---

273 "The European Entrepreneurship Competence Framework (EntreComp)."

274 "Entrepreneurship Teaching Toolkit."

central to the system's design. Creativity and innovation are embedded throughout the educational experience via project-based learning, and collaboration among students is emphasized over competition and standardized testing.[275]

Harvard's Tony Wagner described Finland as perhaps the only country in the world today in which high school students graduate "innovation-ready." He cited the Finnish K-12 educational model as a central reason for which the country is consistently rated as one of the most innovative economies in the world.[276]

In China, billionaire Alibaba co-founder Jack Ma recently exited the business world to focus on re-shaping youth education to meet the demands of the modern era.

"In the industrial era, you had to remember faster, you have to remember more, you have to calculate faster. These are the things machines can now do much better than you," explained Ma. "We have to teach our kids how to be innovative, constructive, and creative so they can survive in the AI (artificial intelligence) period."[277]

China is fortunate to have a visionary leader that not only recognizes the imperative for change, but has committed his vast resources and time to enact this transformation across the country.

---

275 John Kennedy, "Inside a Finnish school: What Finland can teach the world about education."

276 Thomas Friedman, "Need a job? Invent It."

277 Karen Gilchrist, "Why Jack Ma says he'd never get a job at Alibaba today."

Higher Education Considerations

Second, we examined briefly the role that post-secondary education is playing in advancing entrepreneurship coursework.

It turns out that higher education in the U.S. has clearly recognized the need to cultivate the Entrepreneurial Mindset in students and has already adapted its curricula accordingly. A Kaufman Foundation study outlines this progression very clearly.[278]

In 1985, college campuses in the U.S. offered approximately 250 entrepreneurship courses. By 2008, more than 5,000 entrepreneurship courses were being offered in two-year and four-year institutions. Today, well over 400,000 students a year take classes in the subject, with almost 9,000 faculty members. While there is still work to be done, especially in adapting pedagogies to be more project-based and focusing on mindset development, higher learning institutions have made demonstrable strides in this arena.

Jonathan Fay, executive director for the Center for Entrepreneurship at the University of Michigan, summed it up by stating, "Students have recognized a need for the entrepreneurial mindset to provide resiliency in their careers." The Center has seen a sixty-five percent increase in a five-year period.[279] This is just one of literally thousands of examples from across the U.S. of how higher education is responding to modern day demands.

---

278 Arnobio Morelix, "The evolution of entrepreneurship on college campuses."

279 Maria Clara Cobo, "College Towns Are The Next Big Thing For Startups."

Dr. Sethuraman Panchanathan, Chief Innovation Officer at Arizona State University, commented on the topic as follows:

> *As both jobs and entire industries are continually transforming, we now have the chance to completely rethink how we prepare students for the workforce. At ASU, we have found that by focusing on project-based experiential learning, students acquire the qualities that will best equip them for the future of work...creative thinking, adaptability and collaboration across multiple disciplines. Incidentally, these are also qualities most desired by employers.*[280]

Connecting to rapid advancements occurring around the world in youth entrepreneurship education, and to higher education which has made substantial strides in this area, are two key additional focus areas for assembling a comprehensive ecosystem strategy for the movement.

The seventh and final tenet for making Entrepreneurship for All real is that it will take a vast ecosystem working collaboratively to make it happen.

THE EIGHTH WONDER OF THE WORLD

We have now examined each of our seven tenets for crafting the Entrepreneurship for All movement. But there is one more concept to consider before we adjourn.

---

280 Dr. Sethuraman Panchanathan, "Key to Success in the Future of Work? Experiential Learning."

It is what Albert Einstein called the "Eighth Wonder of the World."[281]

The idea goes something like this. The earlier you invest money in assets that pay interest or dividends, the better off you are financially over time.

Why? Because the interest you earn earns interest on itself. With time, this interest earned on interest has a dramatic compounding effect, especially as you look at the impact ten, twenty, or thirty years into the future.

In contrast, what happens if you delay investments in assets that pay interest or dividends? Well, the longer you wait, the more you lose out on the compounding effects. In the worst-case scenario, you defer dividend and interest-bearing investments for so long that you miss out entirely on the benefits of Einstein's "eighth wonder."

Now, let's apply the analogy of compounding interest to the return on investments in youth entrepreneurship education.

In summary, here are the major themes we have explored throughout this book:

1. We have seen how the trajectories of young people's lives can be dramatically altered through project-based entrepreneurship education. The real-life stories of Zoe Damacela, Dagim Girma, and Gabriel Sheikh illustrate how poignant this unique pedagogy can be in transforming young lives.

---

281 "Einstein's Eighth Wonder of the World."

2. We have delved into the pivotal moment that led me to write this book.

3. We have unearthed how the roots of our public K-12 educational systems in the U.S. reside in the Prussian factory model, which was constructed to produce workers for Industrialization. This approach is characterized by principles including a presumption of knowledge scarcity vs. knowledge abundance, an emphasis on convergent thinking vs. divergent thinking, and a focus on preparation for performing repetitive tasks.

4. We have analyzed how the Future of Work is being reshaped by trends including the automation of repetitive tasks and pattern recognition, the Gig Economy, and Conscious Capitalism. These dynamics are resulting in a realignment of the kinds of proficiencies and educational experiences that will be most valuable moving forward.

5. We have examined the eight domains of the Entrepreneurial Mindset and revealed how this ethos empowers people to become "robot-proof" for the Future of Work.

6. We have articulated how the eight elements of the Entrepreneurial Mindset are measured and monitored to drive continuous improvement.

7. We have demonstrated how project-based entrepreneurship education is the quintessential learning method to help young people build the eight domains of the Entrepreneurial Mindset.

8. We have assessed how the business planning project in entrepreneurship education is used to connect students to the "real world" through mentors. The network effects resulting from these mentor relationships further advance young learners' ability to build the Entrepreneurial Mindset early and often.

9. We have chronicled the stories of four heroic teachers of youth entrepreneurship to showcase the central role educators play in delivering the project-based entrepreneurship educational experience.

10. We have codified seven tenets for organizing the Entrepreneurship for All movement. These principles will allow us to bring scale to the development of the Entrepreneurial Mindset for young people and prepare them for the Future of Work in the twenty-first century.

At this point, we have reached a fork in the road. We essentially have two options for how to proceed.

On one hand, we can make excuses for maintaining the status quo. This path would be like delaying decisions to invest in assets that generate interest or dividends. We would miss out on the compounding returns. In effect, we would fail to realize the immense benefits of the "eighth wonder of the world."

Or, we can join forces to accelerate the proliferation of project-based entrepreneurship education to empower our next generations. In this way, we can equip young people with the Entrepreneurial Mindset that is necessary for them to flourish in the Future of Work.

CONCLUSION

With the release of this book, the Entrepreneurship for All movement is officially underway. It is now up to each of us to make it happen, together.

And remember, all proceeds from this book are charitable contributions. So, you can kill two birds with one stone: 1) purchasing books supports NFTE's mission directly, and 2) distributing books to others stimulates the Entrepreneurship for All movement.

Let's go!

#TheEntrepreneurialMindset
#Eship4All

GLOSSARY

Computer Science for All:
Computer Science for All is a national program announced in early 2016 by the Obama Administration Office of Science & Technology Policy, leveraging multiple federal agencies and private sector partners, to ensure that rigorous, inclusive and sustainable Computer Science (CS) education is available to all K-12 students across the U.S.

The imperative to add software development and computer coding skills into U.S. classrooms is one of the most significant education reform movements of the twenty-first century. The initiative places a special emphasis on under-resourced communities, where need is highest.[282]

Many U.S. states and school districts also have their own dedicated Computer Science for All programs. In addition, there is a nonprofit organization based in New York City called CSforALL which brings educators, administrators,

---

282 "CS for All."

school boards, departments of education, researchers, and industry partners together to advance the Computer Science for All movement.[283]

Conscious Capitalism:

Conscious Capitalism is a guiding principle espousing that companies should consider purpose-driven value creation holistically across the full range of their six major stakeholders—customers, employees, suppliers, communities, the environment, and shareholders.[284] Conscious Capitalism stands in contrast to the view proclaimed by Nobel Prize-winning economist Milton Friedman and others that a company's sole purpose is to maximize profits for shareholders.[285]

The heightened level of transparency elicited by the internet, mobile devices, and social media has been a key factor contributing to the rise of a more conscientious version of capitalism by shining a spotlight on both positive and negative effects that corporations have on society. The impact of pandemics such as COVID-19,[286] climate change,[287] and other global threats add further clarity to our need to work together more holistically in the best interest of society.

283 "Join the Movement to Bring Computer Science to ALL Students."

284 Mackey and Sisodia, *Conscious Capitalism,* chap. 2.

285 Milton Friedman, "The Social Responsibility of Business is to Increase its Profits."

286 Borge Brende, "COVID-19 Pandemic Shows We Must Reduce Our Blindspot to Risk."

287 David Introcaso, "Climate Change Is The Greatest Threat To Human Health in History."

The phrase was made popular by Whole Foods founder John Mackey and Babson College professor Raj Sisodia based upon a book they wrote called *Conscious Capitalism*.[288]

Departments of Education for U.S. States:

Each state and territory in the U.S. has a dedicated Department of Education, or its equivalent, which serves as the government organization responsible for education policy, budgeting, and oversight.[289] State-level Departments of Education in the U.S. have a leader overseeing the department. State governors also typically have a high degree of influence on the education policies set forth by each state.[290]

District:

A District is a geographical unit for the local administration of elementary or secondary schools in the U.S. It is a special-purpose government entity that can be administered independently or be dependent on the local government, such as a city or county.[291] In the U.S., there are about 14,000 secondary public-school Districts that operate within the state-level government organizations in which they are located.[292] About 90,000 school board members oversee education policy across these 14,000 Districts.[293]

---

288 Mackey and Sisodia, *Conscious Capitalism*, chap. 1.

289 "State Boards of Education."

290 Sargrad and Partelow, "11 Ways New Governors Can Lead on Education Through Executive Actions."

291 "Public school district."

292 National Center for Education Statistics (Table 214.10).

293 "About Us."

There are also about 3,000 public charter schools[294] and about 13,000 private schools[295] that serve at the secondary education level (ages eleven to eighteen) in the U.S. Taken together, this totals about 30,000 local secondary educational units in the U.S. across public school Districts, charter schools, and private schools.

Entrepreneurial Mindset:

The Entrepreneurial Mindset is a set of attitudes, behaviors and skills characterized by eight domains as follows: Future Orientation, Creativity & Innovation, Comfort with Risk, Communication & Collaboration, Flexibility & Adaptability, Critical Thinking & Problem Solving, Initiative & Self-direction, and Opportunity Recognition. These domains were developed by NFTE based upon extensive research and decades of experience in teaching entrepreneurship at the middle and high school levels in the U.S. and around the world.[296]

Entrepreneurial Mindset Index (EMI):

The EMI is an assessment that measures the eight domains of the Entrepreneurial Mindset in students. Just as the SAT measures certain academic skills, this examination quantifies a student's propensity for entrepreneurial thinking. In practice, the EMI is used to diagnose a student's strengths and weakness in each of the eight domains, generally near the beginning of

---

294 "Key Facts About Charter Schools."

295 National Center for Education Statistics (Table 214.10).

296 "Tools for Life."

an entrepreneurship curriculum element. This diagnostic is then used to personalize learning for each student to build upon strengths and enhance areas of improvement.[297]

Entrepreneurship and Small Business (ESB) Certification:
The ESB certification is built to test and validate foundation-level concepts and knowledge in entrepreneurship and small business management. These core concepts include recognizing and evaluating opportunities; planning for, starting, and operating a business; marketing and sales; and financial management. It is strongly recommended that students attain this broadly recognized industry credential before graduating from high school because it is valuable in both seeking work experience and applying for higher education.[298]

Entrepreneurship for All:
Entrepreneurship for All, Entrepreneurship Education for All, or #Eship4All, is a new movement launched with the release of this book designed to bring rigorous, inclusive and sustainable project-based entrepreneurship education to all middle and high school students across the U.S. and ultimately around the world. The movement places a special emphasis on under-resourced communities, where the need is most acute. In the U.S., the movement aims to leverage best practices from the Computer Science for All program.

---

297 Gold and Rodriguez, "Measuring Entrepreneurial Mindset In Youth: Learnings From NFTE's Entrepreneurial Mindset Index."

298 "Entrepreneurship and Small Business."

Entrepreneurship Pathway:

The Entrepreneurship Pathway is a project-based entrepreneurship education curriculum developed by NFTE to help young people build the Entrepreneurial Mindset. The curriculum includes awareness and exposure programs for middle school students such as Start-Up Tech, Venture, and the World Series of Innovation. For high school students, the major curriculum components include Entrepreneurship 1 & 2, which are ideally suited for completion as full-year courses during their sophomore and junior years. There are also summer school options and modular offerings that can be embedded piecemeal into a school's pre-existing curricula.[299]

Every Student Succeeds Act (ESSA):

The ESSA is a federal law passed in 2015 with bi-partisan support that governs public K-12 education policy in the U.S. One of the bill's most significant features is its requirement that states employ a multiple-measures system of accountability, beyond just standardized testing. The use of these additional indicators provides an opening for innovative states, Districts, and charter schools to build a more holistic approach for students, including investments in developing the Entrepreneurial Mindset through project-based entrepreneurship education.[300]

Future of Work:

The Future of Work is a body of research that examines trends impacting the workplace and forecasts how these dynamics

---

299 "How We Do It."

300 "New education law shifts federal influence over public schools."

will shape the nature of work in the twenty-first century. The increasingly rapid pace of disruption from technologies such as artificial intelligence, machine learning, and robotic process automation, coupled with global threats ranging from pandemics to climate change, have made the Future of Work discourse one of the defining themes of our time. Three trends shaping the Future of Work in the twenty-first century include the automation of repetitive tasks and pattern recognition, the Gig Economy, and Conscious Capitalism.

Gig Economy:

The Gig Economy is characterized by the increasing use of remotely working independent contractors vs. full-time employees to get work done. The upside of these freelance work arrangements is increased freedom, flexibility, and new opportunities to earn supplementary income or even to select this kind of entrepreneurship as a long-term career. The downside is that employers are not required to provide health insurance, retirement benefits, paid time off, or certain legal protections to part-time workers in the U.S.

In 2019, the Gig Economy hit a tipping point. For the first time, fully half of all freelancers indicated that they view independent contracting as a long-term career choice rather than a temporary way to make money as a "side hustle."[301] The emergence of advanced collaboration tools like Zoom and digital platforms such as Upwork, Uber, TaskRabbit, DoorDash, Rover, Care.com, and many others that match

---

301 "Sixth annual 'Freelancing in America' study finds that more people than ever see freelancing as a long-term career path."

labor supply with labor demand efficiently have been key factors contributing to the rise of the Gig Economy.[302]

Industrialization:

Industrialization refers to the transition of an economy from one centered on agriculture to one driven by the manufacturing of goods.[303] In the U.S., Industrialization began in the late eighteenth century with the emergence of factories in order to enable mass production and the organization of labor around assembly lines. The Prussian model for education arose during this period in order to produce workers that were well-suited for factory work. This Prussian method was used as the blueprint for the creation of the U.S. public K-12 educational systems that are still in place today.[304]

Master Educator:

Master Educator is a level that NFTE teachers can reach generally after five or more years of outstanding performance in teaching the Entrepreneurship Pathway curriculum to students. Teachers that attain this ranking are eligible to conduct new teacher training sessions and provide support services to other educators throughout the NFTE network. Master Educators also lead quarterly professional learning community sessions to share best practices with other teachers.[305]

---

302 "Best Gig Economy Apps: 50 Leading Apps to Find Gig Work and Live the Gig Economy Lifestyle."

303 Jim Chappelow, "What Is Industrialization?"

304 Lewis Rincon, "The Development of American Schools."

305 "Recognition and Leadership Opportunities."

Model Teacher Challenge:

The Model Teacher Challenge is an NFTE program that encourages teachers to perform to a consistently high standard that facilitates student achievement and Entrepreneurial Mindset growth. Each year, NFTE identifies the most highly skilled and passionate educators who exemplify sound pedagogical content knowledge, effective classroom management strategies, data-driven decisions, and a belief that the Entrepreneurial Mindset can change a student's life trajectory. Model Teacher Challenge winners receive monetary awards, peer recognition, and access to other leadership opportunities.[306]

Network for Teaching Entrepreneurship (NFTE):

NFTE is a nonprofit organization based in New York City that has reached over 1 million under-resourced students through project-based entrepreneurship education in the U.S. and around the world.[307] Through a network of teachers, students, volunteers, corporate partners, donors, and alumni, NFTE works every day to ignite the Entrepreneurial Mindset in young people. NFTE was founded in 1987 by Brooklyn public school teacher Steve Mariotti when he saw that student engagement was dramatically higher when he experimented with teaching entrepreneurship as compared to more traditional subjects.[308]

---

306 Ibid.

307 "Preparing The Next Generation – 2018 Annual Report."

308 Mariotti and Devi, *Goodbye Homeboy,* preface.

Project-Based Learning (PBL):

PBL is a learning method that encourages students to engage in team-oriented projects set around solving problems to open-ended, real-world challenges. PBL requires teachers to coach more and instruct less, to embrace interdisciplinary learning, and to be more comfortable with ambiguity and discovery during the learning process.[309] Studies indicate that implementing this learning method in schools enables students to develop the kind of mindset required for the modern workplace.[310]

Science, Technology, Engineering, & Mathematics (STEM):

STEM education is based on the idea of teaching students in four specific disciplines—science, technology, engineering, and mathematics. Given the central role that these topics play in our twenty-first century economy, there is widespread consensus that enhanced, age-appropriate STEM curricula are a vital element of preparing young people for the Future of Work.[311]

Sustainable Development Goals (SDGs):

The SDGs are a collection of seventeen global goals designed to be a "blueprint to achieve a better and more sustainable future for all." The SDGs were set forth in 2015 by the United Nations General Assembly with the aim of achieving them by the year 2030.[312] The seventeen goals are as follows:

---

309 "What is PBL?"

310 Ibid.

311 Anna Powers, "Davos Announces That the Highest Growth Careers Are in STEM, With a Caveat."

312 "Sustainable Development Goals."

1) No Poverty, 2) Zero Hunger, 3) Good Health & Well-being, 4) Quality Education, 5) Gender Equality, 6) Clean Water & Sanitation, 7) Affordable & Clean Energy, 8) Decent Work & Economic Growth, 9) Industry, Innovation, & Infrastructure, 10) Reducing Inequality, 11) Sustainable Cities & Communities, 12) Responsible Consumption & Production, 13) Climate Action, 14) Life Below Water, 15) Life On Land, 16) Peace, Justice, & Strong Institutions, 17) Partnerships for the Goals.

Youth Entrepreneurship Challenge:
The Youth Entrepreneurship Challenge is a local, regional, and national business planning competition run by NFTE annually for high school students.[313] Each spring, thousands of students in dozens of states across the U.S. enter the competition and make their pitches to panels of judges. The final group of contestants is invited to New York City for the national finals each fall.

Finalists receive prizes and grants that can be used toward post-secondary education and to help fund their startups. Competitive events such as the Youth Entrepreneurship Challenge, and others like it, that motivate and inspire students are a cornerstone element of the project-based entrepreneurship educational experience.[314]

---

313 "NFTE Youth Entrepreneurship Challenge."

314 Kayla Prochnow, "The Best Entrepreneurship Competitions for K-12 Students."

APPENDIX

Introduction

Aoun, Joseph E., *Robot-Proof: Higher Education in the Age of Artificial Intelligence.* Cambridge: The MIT Press, 2017.

Araya, Daniel. *Rethinking US Education Policy: Paradigms of the Knowledge Economy.* New York: Palgrave Macmillan, 2015.

"Automation Anywhere Predicts It Will Be the World's Largest Digital Employer by 2020, On Track to Deploy Three Million Bots Worldwide." Automation Anywhere. Accessed April 16, 2019. https://www.automationanywhere.com/company/press-room/track-to-deploy-three-million-bots-worldwide.

"Best Gig Economy Apps: 50 Leading Apps to Find Gig Work and Live the Gig Economy Lifestyle." Wonolo. October 11, 2017, https://www.wonolo.com/blog/best-gig-economy-apps.

Brende, Borge. "COVID-19 Pandemic Shows We Must Reduce Our Blindspot to Risk." *Forbes*, March 23, 2020, https://www.forbes.com/sites/worldeconomicforum/2020/03/23/covid-19-pandemic-shows-we-must-reduce-our-blind-spots-to-risk/#520a53cb4688.

Chappelow, Jim. "What is Industrialization?" Investopedia, Last modified July 25, 2019. https://www.investopedia.com/terms/i/industrialization.asp.

Detrixhe, John. "Deutsche Bank's CEO hints that half its workers could be replaced by machines." *Quartz*, November 8, 2017, https://qz.com/1123703/deutsche-bank-ceo-john-cryan-suggests-half-its-workers-could-be-replaced-by-machines/.

Engineering for Kids. "Why is STEM Education so Important?" February 2, 2016. https://www.engineeringforkids.com/about/news/2016/february/why-is-stem-education-so-important-/.

"Future of Work | Singularity U Spain Summit 2019." Singularity University. April 12, 2019. Video, https://www.youtube.com/watch?v=uAdKRvKe5PY&t=1220s.

Giles, Sunnie. "How VUCA Is Reshaping The Business Environment, And What It Means For Innovation." *Forbes*, May 9, 2018, https://www.forbes.com/sites/sunniegiles/2018/05/09/how-vuca-is-reshaping-the-business-environment-and-what-it-means-for-innovation/#5e5e778ceb8d.

Gray, Alex. "The 10 skills you need to thrive in the Fourth Industrial Revolution." *World Economic Forum*, January 19, 2016, https://www.weforum.org/agenda/2016/01/the-10-skills-you-need-to-thrive-in-the-fourth-industrial-revolution/.

"Left Brain vs. Right Brain: What Does This Mean for Me?" Healthline. Accessed March 21, 2020. https://www.healthline.com/health/left-brain-vs-right-brain#staying-sharp.

"How we do it." Network for Teaching Entrepreneurship. Accessed March 20, 2020. https://www.nfte.com/our-programs/.

Introcaso, David. "Climate Change Is The Greatest Threat To Human Health in History." *Health Affairs*, December 19, 2018, https://www.healthaffairs.org/do/10.1377/hblog20181218.278288/full/.

Mackey, John and Sisodia, Raj. *Conscious Capitalism*. Boston: Harvard Business Review Press, 2014.

Markov, Sergey. "Joy Paul Guilford – One of the founders of the Psychology of Creativity." Genvive, June 11, 2017, https://geniusrevive.com/en/joy-paul-guilford-one-of-the-founders-of-the-psychology-of-creativity/.

McRoberts, Sam. "Artificial Intelligence Is Likely to Make a Career in Finance, Medicine or Law a Lot Less Lucrative." *Entrepreneur*, August 11, 2017, https://www.entrepreneur.com/article/295827.

"Measuring Entrepreneurial Mindset In Youth." Network for Teaching Entrepreneurship. Accessed March 17, 2020. https://www.nfte.com/entrepreneurial-mindset/.

Metz, Cade. "Google's AlphaGo Levels Up from Board Games to Power Grids." *Wired Business*, May 24, 2017, https://www.theverge.com/2019/8/9/20799148/darpa-drones-robots-swarm-military-test.

Peters, Jay. "Watch DARPA test out swarms of drones." *The Verge*, August 9, 2019, https://www.theverge.com/2019/8/9/20799148/darpa-drones-robots-swarm-military-test.

"Plus.ai Completes First Cross-Country Commercial Freight Run by a Self-Driving Truck in Record Three Days." Business Wire, December 10, 2019. https://www.businesswire.com/news/home/20191210005309/en/Plus.ai-Completes-Cross-Country-Commercial-Freight-Run-Self-Driving.

Strauss, Valerie. "Nelson Mandela on the power of education." *Washington Post*, December 5, 2013, https://www.washingtonpost.com/news/answer-sheet/wp/2013/12/05/nelson-mandelas-famous-quote-on-education/.

Toffler, Alvin. *Future Shock*. New York: Bantam Books, 1971.

"Tools for Life." Network for Teaching Entrepreneurship. Accessed March 15, 2020. https://www.nfte.com/entrepreneurial-mindset/.

U.S. Department of Labor. "Encouraging Future Innovation: Youth Entrepreneurship Education." accessed March 15, 2020. https://www.dol.gov/odep/pubs/fact/entrepreneurship.htm.

Chapter 1

The Audible. "The Audible Final Presentation in New York | Dagim Girma." January 11, 2015. Video, https://www.youtube.com/watch?v=QjyCALvkJfo&t=60s.

Babson College. "Babson Student Named EY Global Youth Entrepreneur of the Year." Accessed March 21, 2020. https://www.babson.edu/about/news-events/babson-announcements/student-dagim-girma-named-ey-global-youth-entrepreneur-of-the-year/.

Breaking Down the Barriers. "6 Facts About Public Speaking Anxiety." Accessed March 21, 2020. https://bdbcommunication.com/6-facts-about-public-speaking-anxiety/.

Crain's Chicago Business, "Zoe Damacela: An entrepreneur is born." February 4, 2010. Video, https://www.youtube.com/watch?v=OR6ItqPXYNE.

IMDb. "Remember the Titans." Accessed March 21, 2020. https://www.imdb.com/title/tt0210945/.

Prochnow, Kayla. "The Best Entrepreneurship Competitions for K-12 Students." Institute of Competition Sciences, April 17, 2018. https://www.competitionsciences.org/2018/04/17/the-best-entrepreneurship-competitions-for-k-12-students/.

Shoket, Ann. "Introducing the First Ever Cover Reader Star!" *Seventeen*, September 1, 2011, https://www.seventeen.com/celebrity/movies-tv/a16279/pretty-amazing-winner-zoe-damacela/.

Vimeo. "Zoe Damacela on the Tyra Banks Show." December 10, 2010. Video, https://vimeo.com/17677992.

"Winners of NFTE National Youth Entrepreneurship Competition Meet President Obama: Atlantic Philanthropies." The Atlantic Philanthropies. Accessed October 19, 2019. https://www.atlanticphilanthropies.org/news/winners-nfte-national-youth-entrepreneurship-competition-meet-president-obama.

"Youth Entrepreneurship Challenge." Network for Teaching Entrepreneurship. Accessed March 20, 2020. https://www.nfte.com/our-programs/.

Chapter 2

Audi Forum Neckarsulm. "Discovery tours." Accessed March 21, 2020.
https://www.audi.de/de/foren/en/audi-forum-neckarsulm/discovery-tours.html.

Seth, Shobhit. "World's Top 10 Software Companies." *Investopedia*, Last modified
May 5, 2019.
https://www.investopedia.com/articles/personal-finance/121714/worlds-top-10-
software-companies.asp.

Studies Weekly. "The Midwest: People and Characteristics." August 11, 2016, Video,
https://www.youtube.com/watch?v=yHs25PZ5Uf4.

"10 Fairy Tale Castles To Visit in Germany." World of Wanderlust. Accessed March 21, 2020.
http://www.worldofwanderlust.com/10-fairy-tale-castles-to-visit-in-germany/.

Chapter 3

Araya, Daniel. *Rethinking US Education Policy: Paradigms of the Knowledge
Economy.* New York: Palgrave Macmillan, 2015.

"The History of Education." *Forbes.* November 1, 2012. Video, 11:27.
https://www.youtube.com/watch?v=LqTwDDTjb6g&t=426s.

Markov, Sergey. "Joy Paul Guilford–One of the founders of the Psychology of
Creativity." Genvive, June 11, 2017.
https://geniusrevive.com/en/joy-paul-guilford-one-of-the-founders-of-the-
psychology-of-creativity/.

Razumnikova, Olga. "Divergent vs. Convergent Thinking." Encyclopedia of
Creativity, Invention, Innovation and Entrepreneurship, Accessed March 15, 2020.
http://link-springer-com-443.webvpn.fjmu.edu.cn/
referenceworkentry/10.1007%2F978-1-4614-3858-8_362.

Rincon, Lewis. "The Development of American Schools." Sutori, Accessed March 15, 2020.
https://www.sutori.com/story/the-development-of-american-schools--
S8bUuKwKBSJvoXDtrAA11XCo.

Rose, Joel. "How to Break Free of Our 19th-Century Factory-Model Education
System." *The Atlantic*, May 9, 2012,
https://www.theatlantic.com/business/archive/2012/05/how-to-break-free-of-our-
19th-century-factory-model-education-system/256881/.

"Do schools kill creativity?" *TED.* January 6, 2007. Video,
https://www.youtube.com/watch?v=iG9CE55wbtY.

Thompson, Derek. "The Economic History of the Last 2000 Years Part II." *The
Atlantic*, June 20, 2012,
https://www.theatlantic.com/business/archive/2012/06/the-economic-history-of-
the-last-2000-years-part-ii/258762/.

Toffler, Alvin, *Future Shock.* New York: Bantam Books, 1971.

Wilson, Woodrow. "The Meaning of a Liberal Education." *High School Teachers
Association of New York*, *Volume 3*, 1909.
https://en.wikisource.org/wiki/The_Meaning_of_a_Liberal_Education.

Chapter 4

Abril, Danielle. "Coronavirus stimulus package would dramatically change gig worker benefits. Here's how." *Fortune,* March 26, 2020, https://fortune.com/2020/03/26/coronavirus-stimulus-package-independent-contractors-gig-economy-unemployment-benefits-uber-lyft-drivers/.

Anthony, Scott D. and Viguerie, Patrick S. "2018 Corporate Longevity Forecast: Creative Destruction is Accelerating." *Innosight,* Spring 2018, https://www.innosight.com/insight/creative-destruction/.

B Impact Assessment. "The B Impact Assessment." Accessed March 16, 2020. https://bimpactassessment.net/?_ga=2.250866566.1425943427.1584120081-1133084675.1584120081.

Backman, Maurie. "Could COVID-19 Cause a Permanent Shift to Remote Work?" *The Motley Fool,* March 24, 2020, https://www.fool.com/careers/2020/03/24/could-covid-19-cause-a-permanent-shift-to-remote-w.aspx.

Bailey, Allison and Bhalla, Vikram. "Organizing for the Future with Tech, Talent and Purpose." Boston Consulting Group. September 16, 2019. https://www.bcg.com/publications/2019/organizing-future-tech-talent-purpose.aspx.

Bloomberg. "Accenture to sell software that allowed it to cut 40,000 jobs." Last modified January 30, 2019, https://www.livemint.com/companies/news/accenture-to-sell-automation-software-that-allowed-it-to-cut-40-000-jobs-1548768068351.html.

Brende, Borge. "COVID-19 Pandemic Shows We Must Reduce Our Blindspot to Risk." *Forbes,* March 23, 2020, https://www.forbes.com/sites/worldeconomicforum/2020/03/23/covid-19-pandemic-shows-we-must-reduce-our-blind-spots-to-risk/#520a53cb4688.

Business Roundtable. "Business Roundtable Redefines the Purpose of a Corporation to Promote an Economy That Serves All Americans." August 19, 2019. https://www.businessroundtable.org/business-roundtable-redefines-the-purpose-of-a-corporation-to-promote-an-economy-that-serves-all-americans.

Certified B Corporation. "About B Corporations." Accessed March 16, 2020. https://bcorporation.net/about-b-corps?fbclid=IwAR3QgdZOO_8kgPHajkYTnKUTOq6dqJFFwMmIn9OytZygtpdpCQg4kw6cq5k.

Certified B Corporation. "How many Certified B Corps are there around the world?" Accessed March 16, 2020. https://bcorporation.net/faq-item/how-many-certified-b-corps-are-there-around-world.

Chasan, Emily. "Tesla's First Impact Report Puts Hard Number on CO2 Emission." *Bloomberg,* April 17, 2019, https://www.bloomberg.com/news/articles/2019-04-17/tesla-s-first-impact-report-puts-hard-number-on-co2-emissions.

Condon, Stephanie. "Amazon offers retailers access to the tech behind Amazon Go." *ZDNet,* March 9, 2020, https://www.zdnet.com/article/amazon-offers-retailers-access-to-the-tech-behind-amazon-go/.

Cone. "Cone Communications Millennial CSR Study." 2015. https://www.conecomm.com/research-blog/2015-cone-communications-millennial-csr-study.

Deloitte. "Millennials want business to shift its purpose." 2016. https://www2.deloitte.com/us/en/pages/about-deloitte/articles/millennials-shifting-business-purpose.html.

Fingas, John. "IBM's Watson AI saved a woman from leukemia." *Engadget*, August 7, 2016, https://www.engadget.com/2016/08/07/ibms-watson-ai-saved-a-woman-from-leukemia/.

Fink, Larry. "Profit & Purpose." Blackrock. Accessed March 16, 2020. https://www.blackrock.com/americas-offshore/2019-larry-fink-ceo-letter.

Friedman, Milton. "The Social Responsibility of Business is to Increase its Profits." *New York Times Magazine*, September 13, 1971, http://umich.edu/~thecore/doc/Friedman.pdf.

"Future of Work | Singularity U Spain Summit 2019." Singularity University. April 12, 2019. Video, https://www.youtube.com/watch?v=uAdKRvKe5PY&t=1220s

Grimes, Shaunta. "It is not the strongest that survives." *Medium*, March 23, 2019, https://medium.com/the-1000-day-mfa/it-is-not-the-strongest-that-survives-973a39f0d026.

Innosight. "Creative Destruction Whips through Corporate America." Winter 2012. https://www.innosight.com/wp-content/uploads/2016/08/creative-destruction-whips-through-corporate-america_final2015.pdf.

Introcaso, David. "Climate Change Is The Greatest Threat To Human Health in History." *Health Affairs*, December 19, 2018, https://www.healthaffairs.org/do/10.1377/hblog20181218.278288/full/.

Josephs, Leslie. "UPS wins first broad FAA approval for drone delivery." *CNBC*, Last modified October 1, 2019, https://www.cnbc.com/2019/10/01/ups-wins-faa-approval-for-drone-delivery-airline.html.

Kessler, Sarah. *Purpose: The End of the Job and the Future of Work*. New York: St. Martin's Press, 2018.

Mackey, John and Sisodia, Raj. *Conscious Capitalism*. Boston: Harvard Business Review Press, 2014.

Manville, Brook. "How To Get The Smartest People In The World To Work For You." *Forbes*, July 24, 2015, https://www.forbes.com/sites/brookmanville/2015/07/24/how-to-get-the-smartest-people-in-the-world-to-work-for-you/#45469b142f21.

Manyika, James and Chui, Michael. "Harnessing automation for a future that works." *McKinsey Global Institute*, January 2017, https://www.mckinsey.com/featured-insights/digital-disruption/harnessing-automation-for-a-future-that-works.

Mayersohn, Nathaniel. "Walmart is doubling down on robot janitors. Here's why." *CNN Business*, Last modified April 9, 2019, https://www.cnn.com/2019/04/09/business/walmart-robots-retail-jobs/index.html.

McKinsey Quarterly. "Getting ready for the future of work." September 2017, https://www.mckinsey.com/business-functions/organization/our-insights/getting-ready-for-the-future-of-work.

Raphael, Rina. "Meatless burgers vs. beef: How Beyond Meat's environmental impact stacks up." *Fast Company*, September 26, 2018, https://www.fastcompany.com/90241836/meatless-burgers-vs-beef-how-beyond-meats-environmental-impact-stacks-up.

Reinvent. "The Future is Freelancing, Says Upwork's CEO." September 15, 2017. Video, https://www.youtube.com/watch?v=Hb2kSCndYvo.

Renshaw, Ben. *Purpose: The extraordinary benefits of focusing on what matters most.* New York: LID Publishing, 2018.

"Seeking responsible leadership." Accenture. Accessed March 16, 2020. https://www.accenture.com/us-en/insights/consulting/responsible-leadership.

Upwork. "Sixth annual 'Freelancing in America' study finds that more people than ever see freelancing as a long-term career path." October 3, 2019. https://www.upwork.com/press/2019/10/03/freelancing-in-america-2019/.

Wonolo. "Best Gig Economy Apps: 50 Leading Apps to Find Gig Work and Live the Gig Economy Lifestyle." October 11, 2017, https://www.wonolo.com/blog/best-gig-economy-apps.

Chapter 5

Aoun, Joseph E., *Robot-Proof: Higher Education in the Age of Artificial Intelligence.* Cambridge: The MIT Press, 2017.

Anderson, Bruce. "The Most In-Demand Hard and Soft Skills of 2020," *LinkedIn Learning*, January 9, 2020, https://business.linkedin.com/talent-solutions/blog/trends-and-research/2020/most-in-demand-hard-and-soft-skills.

Anthony, Scott D. and Viguerie, Patrick S. "2018 Corporate Longevity Forecast: Creative Destruction is Accelerating." *Innosight*, Spring 2018, https://www.innosight.com/insight/creative-destruction/.

BBC News. "Go master quits because AI 'cannot be defeated'," November 27, 2019, https://www.bbc.com/news/technology-50573071.

Brende, Borge. "COVID-19 Pandemic Shows We Must Reduce Our Blindspot to Risk." *Forbes*, March 23, 2020, https://www.forbes.com/sites/worldeconomicforum/2020/03/23/covid-19-pandemic-shows-we-must-reduce-our-blind-spots-to-risk/#520a53cb4688.

Colvin, Geoffrey. *Humans are Underrated: What High Achievers Know That Brilliant Machines Never Will.* New York: Penguin, 2015.

Friedman, Thomas. "Need a job? Invent It." *New York Times*, March 30, 2013, https://www.nytimes.com/2013/03/31/opinion/sunday/friedman-need-a-job-invent-it.html.

Giles, Sunnie. "How VUCA Is Reshaping The Business Environment, And What It Means For Innovation." *Forbes*, May 9, 2018, https://www.forbes.com/sites/sunniegiles/2018/05/09/how-vuca-is-reshaping-the-business-environment-and-what-it-means-for-innovation/#5e5e778ceb8d.

Gray, Alex. "The 10 skills you need to thrive in the Fourth Industrial Revolution." *World Economic Forum*, January 19, 2016, https://www.weforum.org/agenda/2016/01/the-10-skills-you-need-to-thrive-in-the-fourth-industrial-revolution/.

Healthline. "How COVID-19 Could Affect Kids' Long-Term Social Development." Accessed April 11, 2020. https://www.healthline.com/health-news/social-distancing-effects-on-social-development.

IBM. "IBM 2010 Global CEO Study: Creativity Selected as Most Crucial Factor for Future Success." May 18, 2010. https://www.ibm.com/news/ca/en/2010/05/20/v384864m81427w34.html.

Innosight. "Creative Destruction Whips through Corporate America." Winter 2012. https://www.innosight.com/wp-content/uploads/2016/08/creative-destruction-whips-through-corporate-america_final2015.pdf.

Introcaso, David. "Climate Change Is The Greatest Threat To Human Health in History." *Health Affairs*, December 19, 2018, https://www.healthaffairs.org/do/10.1377/hblog20181218.278288/full/.

Klebikov, Sergei. "Microsoft Is Winning The 'Cloud War' Against Amazon: Report." *Forbes*, January 7, 2020, https://www.forbes.com/sites/sergeiklebnikov/2020/01/07/microsoft-is-winning-the-cloud-war-against-amazon-report/#2243da4c3bec.

Mackey, John and Sisodia, Raj. *Conscious Capitalism*. Boston: Harvard Business Review Press, 2014.

Mauri, Terence. "Want To Think Like Satya Nadella? Follow 3 Simple Rules." *Inc. Magazine*, February 4, 2019, https://www.inc.com/terence-mauri/how-satya-nadella-uses-learn-it-all-to-beat-know-it-all.html.

McKinsey Quarterly. "Getting ready for the future of work." September, 2017, https://www.mckinsey.com/business-functions/organization/our-insights/getting-ready-for-the-future-of-work.

Network for Teaching Entrepreneurship. "NFTE Releases New Research on Measuring Entrepreneurial Thinking in Young People." November 28, 2018. https://www.nfte.com/wp-content/uploads/2018/12/NFTE-releases-new-research-on-measuring-entrepreneurial-mindset-in-youth-12042018.pdf.

Network for Teaching Entrepreneurship. "Tools for Life." Accessed March 15, 2020. https://www.nfte.com/entrepreneurial-mindset/.

PWC. "The talent challenge: Harnessing the power of human skills in the machine age." 2017. https://www.pwc.com/gx/en/ceo-survey/2017/deep-dives/ceo-survey-global-talent.pdf.

Quote Investigator. "It Is Not the Strongest of the Species that Survives But the Most Adaptable to Change." May 4, 2014. https://quoteinvestigator.com/2014/05/04/adapt/.

Rainie, Lee and Anderson, Janna. "The Future of Jobs and Jobs Training." *Pew Research Center,* May 3, 2017, https://www.pewresearch.org/internet/2017/05/03/the-future-of-jobs-and-jobs-training/.

Schwantes, Marcel. "3 Big Future of Work Trends Every Leader Should Know About." *Inc.*, February, 11, 2020, https://www.inc.com/marcel-schwantes/3-big-trends-about-future-of-work-every-leader-should-know-about.html.

Solis, Brian. "Digital Darwinism: How Disruptive Technology Is Changing Business For Good." *Wired,* Accessed March 17, 2020, https://www.wired.com/insights/2014/04/digital-darwinism-disruptive-technology-changing-business-good/.

Summers, Lawrence. "Will 2015 be the year of jobless growth?," *World Economic Forum,* November 7, 2014, https://www.weforum.org/agenda/2014/11/will-2015-year-jobless-growth/.

United Nations. "Sustainable Development Goals." Accessed March 17, 2020. https://sustainabledevelopment.un.org/?menu=1300.

Weinberger, Mark. "How new mindsets and diversity are shaping the future of work." EY, April 25, 2018. https://www.ey.com/en_us/workforce/how-new-mindsets-and-diversity-are-defining-the-future-of-work.

Chapter 6

American Psychology Association. "Industrial and Organizational Psychology." Accessed March 17, 2020. https://www.apa.org/ed/graduate/specialize/industrial.

Anderson, Bruce. "The Most In-Demand Hard and Soft Skills of 2020," *LinkedIn Learning,* January 9, 2020, https://business.linkedin.com/talent-solutions/blog/trends-and-research/2020/most-in-demand-hard-and-soft-skills.

Gold, Thomas and Rodriguez, Sophia. "Measuring Entrepreneurial Mindset In Youth: Learnings From NFTE's Entrepreneurial Mindset Index." Network for Teaching Entrepreneurship, November 2018. http://www.nfte.com/wp-content/uploads/2017/12/NFTE-Whitepaper-Measuring-Entrepreneurial-Mindset-in-Youth-November-2018.pdf.

InformationWeek. "Qualtrics Dominates Academic Survey Research." August 24, 2013, https://www.informationweek.com/qualtrics-dominates-academic-survey research/d/d-id/1110904.

Institute of Psychometric Testing. "Situational judgement tests." Accessed March 17, 2020. https://www.psychometricinstitute.com.au/Situational_judgment_Psychometric_tests.html.

Joelson, Richard. "Locus of control." *Psychology Today,* August 2, 2017, https://www.psychologytoday.com/us/blog/moments-matter/201708/locus-control.

Qualtrics. "Qualtrics Ranked #1 Enterprise Leader for Customer Experience and Employee Experience in Industry-Leading Product Ranking." June 25, 2019. https://www.qualtrics.com/news/qualtrics-ranked-1-enterprise-leader-for-customer-experience-and-employee-experience-in-industry-leading-product-ranking/.

Qualtrics. "Trusted by over 11,000 of the world's leading brands and 99 of the top 100 business schools." Accessed March 17, 2020. https://www.qualtrics.com/customers/.

Network for Teaching Entrepreneurship. "Eight Educators Advance to Final Round of National Competition in NFTE Model Teacher Challenge." June 17, 2019. https://www.nfte.com/press-releases/eight-educators-advance-to-final-round-in-2019-nfte-model-teacher-challenge/.

Network for Teaching Entrepreneurship. "Expanded Explorations Into The Psychology of Entrepreneurship: Findings From The 2001-2002 Study of NFTE in Two Boston Public High Schools." September 2003. https://www.nfte.com/wp-content/uploads/2017/07/harvard-nfte_study_01-02_full_report.pdf.

Network for Teaching Entrepreneurship. "Measuring Entrepreneurial Thinking." November 28, 2018. http://www.nfte.com/wp-content/uploads/2017/12/NFTE-Whitepaper-Measuring-Entrepreneurial-Mindset-in-Youth-November-2018.pdf.

PR Newswire. "New York on Tech Rebrands to America on Tech to Reflect Its National Expansion." October 16, 2019, https://www.prnewswire.com/news-releases/new-york-on-tech-rebrands-to-america-on-tech-to-reflect-its-national-expansion-300939986.html.

Schaffhauser, Dian. "Measuring Academic and Nonacademic Skills Equally Important." *The Journal: Transforming Education Through Technology*, September 5, 2018, https://thejournal.com/articles/2018/09/05/measuring-academic-and-nonacademic-skills-equally-important.aspx.

Success Via Apprenticeship Program. "Have A Passion For A Trade? Become A CTE Teacher." Accessed March 17, 2020. https://www.svaprogram.org/.

SurveyMonkey. "Learn when and how to use Likert scale questions." accessed March 17, 2020. https://www.surveymonkey.com/mp/likert-scale/.

Chapter 7

Bucks Institute for Education: PBLWorks. "Gold Standard PBL." Accessed March 17,2020. https://www.pblworks.org/what-is-pbl/gold-standard-project-design.

Bucks Institute for Education: PBLWorks. "What is PBL?" Accessed March 17, 2020. https://www.pblworks.org/what-is-pbl.

Burrell, Jackie. "Laws to Remember When You Legally Become an Adult at 18." *Very Well Family*, Last modified July 18, 2019, https://www.verywellfamily.com/happy-18th-birthday-new-adult-3570791.

Carpenter, Colton. "The Divided United States of America." *Harvard Political Review*, March 18, 2019, https://harvardpolitics.com/columns-old/divided-states/.

Certiport. "Entrepreneurship and Small Business." Accessed March 17, 2020. https://certiport.pearsonvue.com/Certifications/ESB/Certification/Overview.aspx.

Gstalter, Morgan. "7 in 10 millennials say they would vote for a socialist." *The Hill*, October 28, 2019, https://thehill.com/homenews/campaign/467684-70-percent-of-millennials-say-theyd-vote-for-a-socialist-poll.

Kaur, Harmeet. "The student loan debt is $1.6 trillion and people are struggling to pay it down." *CNN*, Last modified January 19, 2020, https://www.cnn.com/2020/01/19/us/student-loan-slow-repayment-moodys-trnd/index.html.

Lahey, Jessica. "To Help Students Learn, Engage The Emotions." *New York Times*, May 4, 2016, https://well.blogs.nytimes.com/2016/05/04/to-help-students-learn-engage-the-emotions/.

Mackenzie, Deborah. "Our chance to contain the coronavirus may already be over." *New Scientist*, February 24, 2020, https://www.newscientist.com/article/2234967-covid-19-our-chance-to-contain-the-coronavirus-may-already-be-over/.

Manyika, James and Chui, Michael. "Harnessing automation for a future that works." *McKinsey Global Institute*, January 2017, https://www.mckinsey.com/featured-insights/digital-disruption/harnessing-automation-for-a-future-that-works.

MIT App Inventor. "With MIT App Inventor, anyone can build apps with global impact." Accessed March 17, 2020. https://appinventor.mit.edu/.

Network for Teaching Entrepreneurship. "How we do it." Accessed March 20, 2020. https://www.nfte.com/our-programs/.

Pesce, Nicole Lyn. "Chart shows jaw-dropping wealth gap between millennials and boomers." *New York Post*, December 5, 2019, https://nypost.com/2019/12/05/chart-shows-jaw-dropping-wealth-gap-between-millennials-and-boomers/.

Torres, Roberto. "This program helps high-schoolers find their way to tech." *Technically Philadelphia*, October 25, 2017, https://technical.ly/philly/2017/10/25/sap-nfte-startup-tech-philadephia/.

United Nations. "Sustainable Development Goals." Accessed March 17, 2020. https://sustainabledevelopment.un.org/?menu=1300.

Virtual Job Shadow. "LifePath Career Exploration Course." Accessed March 17, 2020. https://www.virtualjobshadow.com/features/career-exploration-course.

Wellemeyer, James. "One-third of Americans say they need a side gig to pay expenses." *MarketWatch*, Jun 15, 2019, https://www.marketwatch.com/story/even-with-a-hot-labor-market-one-third-of-americans-say-they-need-a-side-gig-to-pay-expenses-2019-06-07.

Chapter 8

Alper, Patty. *Teach to Work: How a Mentor, A Mentee and a Project Can Close The Skills Gap in America.* New York: Routledge, 2017.

Chabad.org. "Maimonides' Eight Levels of Charity - Mishneh Torah, Laws of Charity, 10:7–14." Judaism, May 31, 2002. https://www.chabad.org/library/article_cdo/aid/45907/jewish/Eight-Levels-of-Charity.htm.Cue Career.

"Freshman Intern Interviews Riana about UX Design Career." Accessed March 19, 2020. Video, https://www.youtube.com/watch?v=R_AkCEq1ELs&t=268s.

Fin Aid. "Student Loan Debt Clock." Accessed March 22, 2020. https://www.finaid.org/loans/studentloandebtclock.phtml.

Friedman, Zach. "Student Loan Debt Statistics In 2020: A Record $1.6 Trillion." *Forbes,* February 3, 2020, https://www.forbes.com/sites/zackfriedman/2020/02/03/student-loan-debt-statistics/#69dae40d281f.

Holy Trinity High School. "Summer Programs." Accessed March 19, 2020. https://holytrinity-hs.org/academics/summer-programs/.

Horn, Michael and Moesta, Bob. *Choosing College: How To Make Better Learning Decisions Throughout Your Life.* San Francisco: Jossey-Bass, 2019.

Influencive. "Our Education System Is Broken...And 3 Ways To Fix It." July 21, 2018, https://www.influencive.com/our-education-system-is-broken-heres-what-we-need-to-do-to-fix-it/.

Krupnick, Matt. "U.S. Goes To School For Apprenticeships." *U.S. News & World Report,* Septermber 27, 2016, https://www.usnews.com/news/best-countries/articles/2016-09-27/what-europe-can-teach-the-us-about-apprenticeships.

Network for Teaching Entrepreneurship. "Patty Alper Honored With NFTE Lifetime Volunteer Achievement Award." October 12, 2018. https://www.nfte.com/patricia-alper-honored-at-2018-national-entrepreneurship-youth-challenge/.

Network for Teaching Entrepreneurship. "Recognition and Leadership Opportunities." Accessed March 20, 2020. https://www.nfte.com/recognition-and-leadership-opportunities/.

Network for Teaching Entrepreneurship. "Two Top Businesses in Los Angeles Metro Youth Entrepreneurship Challenge Will Go to Nationals." May 24, 2019. https://www.nfte.com/top-two-businesses-in-los-angeles-metro-youth-entrepreneurship-challenge-will-go-to-nationals/.

Singletary, Michelle. "There seems to be no end to the rise in student load debt." *Washington Post,* September 12, 2019, https://www.washingtonpost.com/business/2019/09/12/whos-blame-massive-amount-student-loan-debt-america/.

Slalom. "Redefine what's possible." Accessed March 19, 2020. https://www.slalom.com/home.

UXPA International. "User Experience Professionals Association." Accessed March 19, 2020. https://uxpa.org/.

Van Atta, Alex. "How Slalom and NFTE Used AI and Machine Learning to Mentor High School Entrepreneurs." *Medium*, June 18, 2019, https://medium.com/slalom-technology/how-slalom-and-nfte-used-ai-and-machine-learning-to-mentor-high-school-entrepreneurs-39b17dc6af88.

Yahoo Finance. "Slalom's Alex Van Atta Named Entrepreneurship Volunteer of the Year." May 21, 2019, https://finance.yahoo.com/news/slaloms-alex-van-atta-named-140500466.html.

Youth.gov. "Challenges and Lessons Learned." Accessed March 19, 2020. https://youth.gov/youth-topics/mentoring/challenges-and-lessons-learned-mentoring-relationships.

Chapter 9

60 Minutes. "Tom Brady's favorite Super Bowl ring? 'The next one.'" Jan 30, 2019. Video, https://www.youtube.com/watch?v=ypELsuR1MRM.

Bearn, Suzanne. "How technology has transformed the travel industry." *The Guardian*, February 29, 2016, https://www.theguardian.com/media-network/2016/feb/29/technology-internet-transformed-travel-industry-airbnb.

Mariotti, Steve and Devi, Debra. *Goodbye Homeboy: How My Students Drove Me Crazy and Inspired a Movement*. Dallas: BenBella, 2019.

National Weather Service. "Hurricane Hugo." Accessed March 19, 2020. https://www.weather.gov/ilm/hurricanehugo.

Network for Teaching Entrepreneurship. "Miami Educator Wins Cash Prize in NFTE Model Teacher Challenge." July 12, 2018. https://www.nfte.com/press-releases/miami-educator-wins-cash-prize-in-nfte-model-teacher-challenge/.

Network for Teaching Entrepreneurship. "Preparing The Next Generation – Annual Report." 2018. https://www.nfte.com/wp-content/uploads/2019/02/NFTE-2018-Annual-Report-released-January-2019.pdf.

Network for Teaching Entrepreneurship. "Recognition and Leadership Opportunities." Accessed March 20, 2020. https://www.nfte.com/recognition-and-leadership-opportunities/.

Normandy Schools Collaborative. "Coley Selected as 2018 Global Enterprising Educator." Accessed March 19, 2020. https://www.normandysc.org/site/default.aspx?PageType=3&DomainID=4&ModuleInstanceID=15&ViewID=6446EE88-D30C-497E-9316-3F8874B3E108&RenderLoc=0&FlexDataID=2071&PageID=1.

Wright, Colleen. "'You have to love what you do.' Meet Miami-Dade's four teacher of the year finalists." *Miami Herald*, January 23, 2019, https://www.miamiherald.com/news/local/education/article224644050.html.

Chapter 10

Advocacy Coalition. "2019 State of Computer Science Education: Equity and Diversity." Accessed March 19, 2020. https://advocacy.code.org/2019_state_of_cs.pdf.

Ballotpedia. "United States school districts." Accessed March 19, 2020. https://ballotpedia.org/United_States_school_districts.

Bunting, Joe. "Why You Can't Finish Writing Your Book." The Write Practice, Accessed March 19, 2020. https://thewritepractice.com/cant-finish-writing/.

Civil Rights Data Collection. "Wide-Ranging Education Access And Equity Data Collected From Our Nation's Public Schools." Accessed March 19, 2020. https://ocrdata.ed.gov/.

Clear Wealth Asset Management. "Einstein's Eighth Wonder Of The World." Accessed March 20, 2020. https://www.clearwealthasset.com/einsteins-8th-wonder-of-the-world/.

Cobo, Maria Clara. "College Towns Are The Next Big Thing For Startups." *Forbes*, June 25, 2019, https://www.forbes.com/sites/mariaclaracobo/2019/06/25/college-towns-are-the-next-big-thing-for-startups/#42a5da793b76.

Coburn, Cynthia. "Rethinking Scale: Moving Beyond Numbers to Deep and Lasting Change." *Educational Researcher 32*, no. 6, September 2003. https://www.sesp.northwestern.edu/docs/publications/139042460457c9a8422623f.pdf.

Collins, Jim and Porras, Jerry. *Built to Last: Successful Habits of Visionary Companies*. New York: HarperCollins, 2002.

Community College Daily. "The U.S. Department of Education and the Workforce." June 21, 2018. http://www.ccdaily.com/2018/06/u-s-department-education-workforce/.

CSforALL. "Join the Movement to Bring Computer Science to ALL Students." Accessed March 19, 2020. https://www.csforall.org/.

CSforALL. "Project and Programs: Member Directory." Accessed March 20, 2020. https://www.csforall.org/projects_and_programs/member_directory/.

Embedding Entrepreneurship Education. "Entrepreneurship Teaching Toolkit." Accessed March 20, 2020. https://www.eee-platform.eu/entrepreneurship-teaching-toolkit/.

English, Cynthia. "Parents, Students Want Computer Science Education in School." *Gallup*, August 20, 2015, https://news.gallup.com/poll/184637/parents-students-computer-science-education-school.aspx.

European Union. "The European Entrepreneurship Competence Framework (EntreComp)." Accessed March 20, 2020. https://ec.europa.eu/social/main.jsp?catId=1317&langId=en.

Friedman, Thomas. "Need a job? Invent It." *New York Times*, March 30, 2013, https://www.nytimes.com/2013/03/31/opinion/sunday/friedman-need-a-job-invent-it.html.

Gilchrist, Karen. "Why Jack Ma says he'd never get a job at Alibaba today." *CNBC*, October 20, 2019, https://www.cnbc.com/2019/10/21/why-jack-ma-says-hed-never-get-a-job-at-alibaba-today.html.

In Perspective. "Key Facts About Charter Schools." Last modified 2018. http://www.in-perspective.org/pages/introduction.

Institute of Competition Sciences. "Intel International Science and Engineering Fair." Accessed March 20, 2020. https://www.competitionsciences.org/competitions/intel-international-science-and-engineering-fair/.

Intel Education K-12 Resources. "Design and Discovery." Accessed March 19, 2020. https://www.intel.com/content/dam/www/program/education/us/en/documents/K12/design-and-discovery/dd-implementation-examples.pdf.

Kennedy, John. "Inside a Finnish school: What Finland can teach the world about education." *Silicon Republic*, December 15, 2017, https://www.siliconrepublic.com/careers/finland-education-schools-slush.

Morelix, Arnobio. "The evolution of entrepreneurship on college campuses." Kauffman Foundation, Accessed March 20, 2020. https://www.kauffman.org/currents/the-evolution-of-entrepreneurship-on-college-campuses/.

Nation of Makers. "NOMCON 2018 Keynote: Ruthe Farmer." September 17, 2018. Video, https://www.youtube.com/watch?v=gTd_z82ZDdQ&t=2s.

National Association of State Boards of Education. "State Boards of Education." Accessed March 20, 2020. http://www.nasbe.org/.

National Center for Education Statistics (Table 214.10; Accessed March 19, 2020). https://nces.ed.gov/programs/digest/d18/tables/dt18_214.10.asp?current=yes.

National Center for Education Statistics (Table 235.10; Accessed March 20, 2020). https://nces.ed.gov/programs/digest/d17/tables/dt17_235.10.asp.

National Governors Association. "NGA Meetings." Accessed March 20, 2020. https://www.nga.org/about/meetings/.

National School Boards Association. "About Us." Accessed March 19, 2020. https://www.nsba.org/About.

National Science Foundation. "CS for All." Accessed March 19, 2020. https://www.nsf.gov/news/special_reports/csed/csforall.jsp.

The Obama White House. "Champions of Change: Tech Inclusion." July 31, 2013. Video, https://www.youtube.com/watch?v=RXZbWwHWF5U&t=946s.

O'Brien, Anne. "5 Ways ESSA Impacts Standardized Testing." *Edutopia*, January 28, 2016, https://www.edutopia.org/blog/5-ways-essa-impacts-standardized-testing-anne-obrien.

Panchanathan, Dr. Sethuraman. "Key to Success in the Future of Work? Experiential Learning." *Medium*, May 17, 2018, https://medium.com/@DrPanch/key-to-success-in-the-future-of-work-experiential-learning-78b8aea3db07.

PBS News Hour. "New education law shifts federal influence over public schools." December 10, 2015, https://www.pbs.org/newshour/show/new-education-law-shifts-federal-influence-over-public-schools.

Powers, Anna. "Davos Announces That The Highest Growth Careers Are In STEM, With A Caveat." *Forbes*, January 25, 2020, https://www.forbes.com/sites/annapowers/2020/01/25/davos-announces-that-the-highest-growth-careers-are-in-stem-with-a-caveat/#499d11d12921.

Prochnow, Kayla. "The Best Entrepreneurship Competitions for K-12 Students." Institute of Competition Sciences, April 17, 2018. https://www.competitionsciences.org/2018/04/17/the-best-entrepreneurship-competitions-for-k-12-students/.

Sargrad, Scott and Partelow, Lisette. "11 Ways New Governors Can Lead on Education Through Executive Actions." Center for American Progress, January 10, 2019. https://www.americanprogress.org/issues/education-k-12/reports/2019/01/10/464818/11-ways-new-governors-can-lead-education-executive-actions/.

U.S. Congresswoman Grace Meng. "Congresswoman introduces twenty-first Century Youth Entrepreneurship Act following Global Entrepreneurship Week." November 26, 2019. https://meng.house.gov/media-center/press-releases/meng-introduces-legislation-to-help-young-people-become-next-generation.

U.S. Department of Education. "The Federal Role in Education." Accessed March 20, 2020. https://www2.ed.gov/about/overview/fed/role.html.

Glossary

Ballotpedia. "United States school districts." Accessed March 19, 2020. https://ballotpedia.org/United_States_school_districts.

Brende, Borge. "COVID-19 Pandemic Shows We Must Reduce Our Blindspot to Risk." *Forbes*, March 23, 2020, https://www.forbes.com/sites/worldeconomicforum/2020/03/23/covid-19-pandemic-shows-we-must-reduce-our-blind-spots-to-risk/#520a53cb4688.

Chappelow, Jim. "What is Industrialization?" Investopedia, Last modified July 25, 2019. https://www.investopedia.com/terms/i/industrialization.asp.

"Entrepreneurship and Small Business." Certiport. Accessed March 17, 2020. https://certiport.pearsonvue.com/Certifications/ESB/Certification/Overview.aspx.

Gold, Thomas and Rodriguez, Sophia. *Measuring Entrepreneurial Mindset In Youth: Learnings From NFTE's Entrepreneurial Mindset Index.* Network for Teaching Entrepreneurship, November 2018. http://www.nfte.com/wp-content/uploads/2017/12/NFTE-Whitepaper-Measuring-Entrepreneurial-Mindset-in-Youth-November-2018.pdf.

In Perspective. "Key Facts About Charter Schools." Last modified 2018. http://www.in-perspective.org/pages/introduction.

Introcaso, David. "Climate Change Is The Greatest Threat To Human Health in History." *Health Affairs*, December 19, 2018, https://www.healthaffairs.org/do/10.1377/hblog20181218.278288/full/

Mariotti, Steve and Devi, Debra. *Goodbye Homeboy: How My Students Drove Me Crazy and Inspired a Movement.* Dallas: BenBella, 2019.

National Center for Education Statistics (Table 214.10) Accessed March 19, 2020. https://nces.ed.gov/programs/digest/d18/tables/dt18_214.10.asp?current=yes.

National School Boards Association. "About Us." Accessed March 19, 2020. https://www.nsba.org/About.

Network for Teaching Entrepreneurship. "How we do it." Accessed March 20, 2020. https://www.nfte.com/our-programs/.

Network for Teaching Entrepreneurship. "Preparing The Next Generation – Annual Report." 2018. https://www.nfte.com/wp-content/uploads/2019/02/NFTE-2018-Annual-Report-released-January-2019.pdf.

Network for Teaching Entrepreneurship. "Recognition and Leadership Opportunities." Accessed March 20, 2020. https://www.nfte.com/recognition-and-leadership-opportunities/.

Network for Teaching Entrepreneurship. "Tools for Life." Accessed March 15, 2020. https://www.nfte.com/entrepreneurial-mindset/.

Network for Teaching Entrepreneurship. "Youth Entrepreneurship Challenge." Accessed March 20, 2020. https://www.nfte.com/our-programs/

PBS News Hour. "New education law shifts federal influence over public schools." December 10, 2015, https://www.pbs.org/newshour/show/new-education-law-shifts-federal-influence-over-public-schools.

Powers, Anna. "Davos Announces That The Highest Growth Careers Are In STEM, With A Caveat." *Forbes*, January 25, 2020, https://www.forbes.com/sites/annapowers/2020/01/25/davos-announces-that-the-highest-growth-careers-are-in-stem-with-a-caveat/#499d11d12921.

Prochnow, Kayla. "The Best Entrepreneurship Competitions for K-12 Students." Institute of Competition Sciences, April 17, 2018. https://www.competitionsciences.org/2018/04/17/the-best-entrepreneurship-competitions-for-k-12-students/.

Rincon, Lewis. "The Development of American Schools." Sutori, Accessed March 15, 2020. https://www.sutori.com/story/the-development-of-american-schools--S8bUuKwKBSJvoXDtrAA11XCo.

Sargrad, Scott and Partelow, Lisette. "11 Ways New Governors Can Lead on Education Through Executive Actions." Center for American Progress, January 10, 2019. https://www.americanprogress.org/issues/education-k-12/reports/2019/01/10/464818/11-ways-new-governors-can-lead-education-executive-actions/.

United Nations. "Sustainable Development Goals." Accessed March 17, 2020. https://sustainabledevelopment.un.org/?menu=1300.

Upwork. "Sixth annual 'Freelancing in America' study finds that more people than ever see freelancing as a long-term career path." October 3, 2019. https://www.upwork.com/press/2019/10/03/freelancing-in-america-2019/.

"What is PBL?" Bucks Institute for Education: PBLWorks. Accessed March 17, 2020. https://www.pblworks.org/what-is-pbl.

Wonolo. "Best Gig Economy Apps: 50 Leading Apps to Find Gig Work and Live the Gig Economy Lifestyle." October 11, 2017, https://www.wonolo.com/blog/best-gig-economy-apps.

CPSIA information can be obtained
at www.ICGtesting.com
Printed in the USA
LVHW020803270720
661604LV00017B/1399